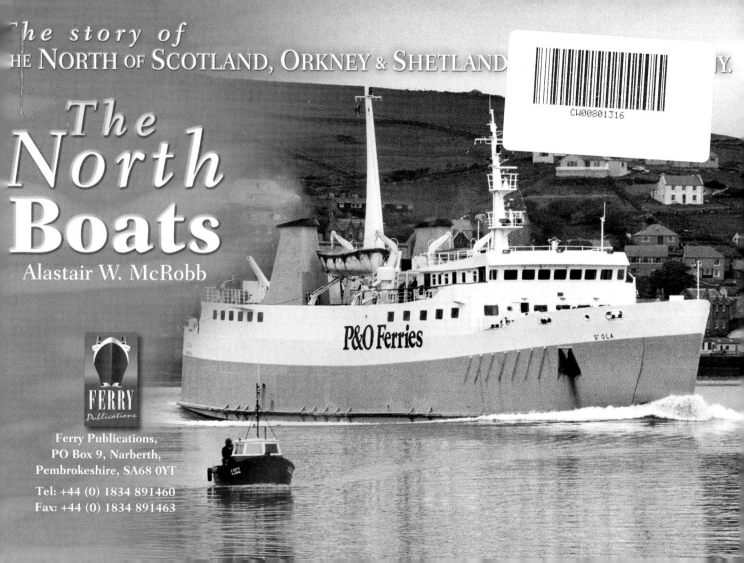

The story of
THE NORTH OF SCOTLAND, ORKNEY & SHETLAND ... Y.

The North Boats

Alastair W. McRobb

Ferry Publications,
PO Box 9, Narberth,
Pembrokeshire, SA68 0YT

Tel: +44 (0) 1834 891460
Fax: +44 (0) 1834 891463

Alastair W. McRobb

Born in 1930 and educated in Aberdeen, before commencing his sea-going career Alastair McRobb served his time in Hall Russell's Ship and Engine Building yards in Aberdeen. His interest in the 'North Boats' emanated from his Shetland-born mother's trips back 'home' during his boyhood days.

After a brief spell as Junior Engineer on foreign going vessels he signed on as 4th Engineer with his beloved North of Scotland, Orkney & Shetland Steam Navigation Company and two years later was serving as relief Chief Engineer on all the company's smaller ships as well as as 2nd Engineer on the larger vessels.

In 1962 he gained his Combined Chief Engineer's Certificate and went on to become Chief Engineer on the *St Ninian* which became his main charge whilst with the Company.

Throughout his life Alastair carried out intensive research on the historical background of the 'North Boats' as well as having a collection of over fifty years' press cuttings, slides, photographs and memorabilia which are now housed in Aberdeen Maritime Museum. He contributed up-to-date news of P&O Scottish Ferries and other shipping news to the Coastal Cruising Association's 'Cruising Monthly,' the Clyde River Steamer Club's 'Annual Review,' Ferry Publications' 'European Ferry Scene' (for whom he was the Northern Isles correspondent) and regularly wrote articles for other shipping newsletters and periodicals.

At the time of his sudden and untimely death in August 1998, the text of this book was unfinished and so 'Ferry Publications' asked Alastair's friend Ian Somerville to write the final section from 1974 until the present day.

A young Alastair McRobb in the engine room of the *St. Magnus* (III) on 30th July 1960. (*A W McRobb collection*)

Alastair McRobb was an expert in his own field regarding the 'North Boats.' Scott Colgate, Marketing Director of P&O Scottish Ferries said of him, "Alastair's knowledge of our Company and his tireless interest and enthusiasm will never be replaced and I will miss him as a source of information. I doubt if anyone knew as much about our Company history as Alastair ... an engineer of the 'old school,' extremely able and well respected and one whose work was also his hobby."

Foreword by Terry Cairns, Managing Director, P&O Scottish Ferries.

Arthur Anderson, co-founder with Brodie McGhie Willcox of the Peninsular and Oriental Steam Navigation Company, was born near Lerwick, Capital of Shetland. We at P&O Scottish Ferries are immensely proud of both our maritime heritage and of the lifeline service provided by the Company and its predecessors to isolated communities in the North of Scotland, Orkney and Shetland.

The sea areas in which we operate are among the most challenging around Britain, particularly in winter. The safety of our passengers, crew and ships is our prime responsibility and is never compromised. We have a thoroughly professional team of people at P&O Scottish Ferries, with many years experience of operations in a sometimes hostile environment. Their commitment is much appreciated by the Board of Directors.

For anyone with a remote interest in the sea and ships or in the Northern Isles, this book (which is enhanced by its unrivalled collection of historic photographs) will hold an instant fascination and P&O Scottish Ferries is delighted to have the opportunity to sponsor it.

We are additionally pleased that the author is one of our former chief engineers whose knowledge, understanding and interest in our Company was second to none. Sadly, Alastair McRobb died before his book could be published, but we hope that readers, both far and wide, will enjoy his text and be tempted to experience our ships and services for themselves.

Mr. Terry Cairns, the Managing Director of P&O Scottish Ferries.

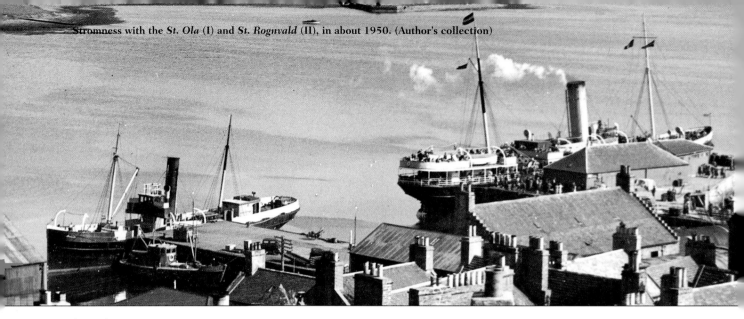

Stromness with the *St. Ola* (I) and *St. Rognvald* (II), in about 1950. (Author's collection)

There are many ferry companies now trading which can trace their history and origins back for lengthy periods of a century and more but whose public image has largely been lost through amalgamations, takeovers, relocations, and in some cases changes in company structure and activity. Perhaps the most decisive act in this loss of public perception has been the change in nomenclature employed for the ships by many of today's ferry companies. The work of consultants, PR departments and marketing strategies is today apparently an essential requirement to present a 'corporate image' but they have all contributed in today's public ignorance of what came before.

Younger members of society can be forgiven for being unaware of the fact that much of what is now the UK arm of Stena Line is essentially the inheritor and successor of that which originally traded as the shipping side of the pre-grouping (pre-1923) railway companies from the 1830/40 era, or that P&O Ferries can trace their antecedants back through the Coast Lines Group to numerous Irish Sea ferry routes originating in the 1820/30 era.

It will be argued, and perhaps rightly so in some cases, that a complete restructuring and change of nomenclature was necessary but it is for others to discuss the pros and cons of this complex and perhaps futile argument. However, the subject of this little history is a company which has an unbroken and readily traceable history of over 200 years, through which the majority of its ships have adhered to a system of nomenclature which originated as far back as 1867, much longer than the memory span of anyone living today, a level of continuity which now perhaps might be difficult to find anywhere else.

The Sailing Ship Era - The first three decades

The formation of the company can be traced to 1790, as the Leith & Clyde Shipping Co., possibly only offering a service between these two ports and as this was 32 years prior to the opening of the Caledonian Canal, all vessels had to travel via the Pentland Firth, that notorious stretch of turbulent water. The vessels employed at that time were probably small sailing smacks of around 50/70 tons and the service frequency is unlikely to have been better than weekly.

In 1820, the 'L&C' amalgamated with the Aberdeen, Dundee & Leith Shipping Co., becoming the Aberdeen, Leith, Clyde & Tay Shipping Co., the positioning of 'Aberdeen' at the beginning of the company title presumably reflecting Aberdeen's position as head office and premier port of call, something which has continued until the present. The word 'Tay' was apparently soon dropped as it was perhaps an area which did not figure greatly in the company's activity, and the name which came to be used for some 50 years was the Aberdeen, Leith & Clyde Shipping Co. which was certainly in use by 1824. This was normally shortened to 'AL&C' and interestingly, it was still possible in the 1960s to find saloon silverware embossed thus. Examples are on display in the Aberdeen Maritime Museum.

Little is known of the early smacks but the *Glasgow Packet* was built in 1811 and the *Edinburgh Packet* (simply *Edinburgh* in some accounts) in 1812, both built by A. Hall & Co. of Aberdeen, renowned builders of the Aberdeen clippers. The *Glasgow Packet* is noted as being of 82 tons, somewhat larger than other smacks whose tonnage has been recorded. This early pair presumably operated on the routes signified by their names. For the first three decades of its existence, the 'AL&C' operated only sailing vessels and a

further four decades elapsed before sail finally disappeared from the scene.

By 1824, the 'AL&C' had four main routes and a fleet of eight smacks, three each allocated to the Leith and Glasgow routes and one each to the Liverpool and Rotterdam routes. The frequencies were 4/5 days, weekly, monthly and six weekly respectively. Known vessels in the fleet at this time were the *Clyde*, the *London* (or *London Packet*) and the *Marquis of Huntly* serving Leith, the *Rotterdam Packet* and the *Liverpool Packet* serving their namesake ports, and the *Edinburgh*. Fares in the cabin were 15/- (75p.), 21/- (£1.05), 2.5 Gns. (£2.625) and 3 Gns. (£3.15) respectively, substantial amounts at that time.

The Liverpool service ceased around 1830/31, while the Glasgow route continued for at least another 12 years and these services may have latterly operated via the Caledonian Canal as it had been opened in 1822. The Rotterdam service has not been traced after 1835 but in 1843 there were still seven smacks trading to Leith and Glasgow, and curiously, the *Belmont*, recorded as serving Grangemouth. One of the Glasgow traders was apparently the *Glasgow Packet* (II), or at least her listed tonnage was quoted as less than before, suggesting a replacement vessel of the same name had been introduced at some stage.

Some seventeen sailing vessels have been identified as belonging to the 'AL&C' but there were possibly others. While sail and steam overlapped in the fleet for some 40 years (1821 - 1860) the earliest steamers did not operate in the winter months, the Leith route reverting to sail during the winters up to 1837/8 and the long vulnerable Lerwick route up to 1860. Lerwick was served by the *Marquis of Huntly* (formerly serving Leith) in 1828, the *Aberdeen Packet* in 1838/9 and 1843, the *William Hogarth* between 1848 and 1852 and the *Fairy* from 1852 to 1860. This last named was

The paddle steamer *Sovereign* entering Aberdeen Harbour. She was built in 1836 and was disposed of in 1865.
(Aberdeen Art Gallery & Museum - attributed to Arthur Smith)

probably the largest sailing vessel in the fleet, a topsail schooner of 150 tons and approximating in tonnage to the first two steamers in the fleet.

Early Steam Days

Henry Bell's *Comet* is universally acknowledged as the precursor of powered vessels in UK waters and the first Clyde steamer when she introduced sailings in 1812 between Glasgow, Greenock and Helensburgh, though she did make one foray that year to the West Highlands via the Crinan Canal. That other great Scottish estuary, the Forth, also introduced steamer sailings between Grangemouth and Newhaven (Edinburgh) in 1813, again with the *Comet* which had transferred to the east coast, and when she eventually returned to the west coast in 1819 she became the first West Highland steamer. The Tay was the next area to feel the influence of steam when the *Union* commenced plying on the Dundee to Fife (Woodhaven or Newport-on-Tay) ferry crossing in 1821.

All major Scottish esturial and island areas thus had steamer services, if in some cases very minimal, in place within nine years of the introduction of steam navigation and in the case of the Clyde, some 42 steamboats had been built to work that area by 1820. Open seas were a rather different matter but in 1821, the Leith & Aberdeen Steam Yacht Co. placed the *Tourist* on the route linking the two name ports, her maiden voyage taking place on 24th May. The *Tourist* called at eight intermediate calling places and took around 12/13 hours for the passage, departing from the terminal ports on alternate days.

The 'AL&C' at this time were operating two trips weekly between Aberdeen and Leith with their smacks and anticipating a loss of trade to the steamer ordered a paddle steamer for their own account. This was the *Velocity*, built by Denny's of Dumbarton and engined by the Greenhead Foundry. The *Velocity* was 149 tons gross and 112 feet long (deck) and was bigger than nearly all the Clyde steamers of the period. She arrived in Aberdeen on 2nd July 1821 from the Clyde and made her maiden voyage two days later to Leith. The terminal used was actually the Stone Pier at Newhaven which was about one mile from the harbour at Leith. Both competing companies steamers always appear to have berthed at Newhaven but the smacks normally berthed in Leith itself.

The *Velocity* made the passage south on Mondays, Wednesdays and Fridays, returning on Tuesdays, Thursdays and Saturdays, departing at 06.00 daily and calling at Stonehaven, Montrose, Arbroath, Crail, Anstruther, Elie and Dysart. The *Tourist* operated on a similar basis but always sailing in the opposite direction to the *Velocity*. Both companies appear to have charged similar fares of 21/- (£1.05) cabin and 12/- (60p.) steerage, considerably more than on the smacks, for the single passage while intermediate ports were charged on a pro rata basis. At none of the intermediate ports did the steamer go alongside, passengers being transferred by small boat, a procedure which must have been exciting, if not actually perilous, on occasions.

The 'L&ASY Co.'ordered a second vessel for the trade from the yard of James Lang of Dumbarton. It was intended that this vessel would supplement the *Tourist's* sailings and continue on to Inverness via intermediate ports. The new vessel, the *Brilliant*, was launched on 9th June 1821 and was a vessel of 159 tons gross and 125 feet long (deck). The maiden voyage commenced from Newhaven at 05.00 on 21st August and appears to have been a direct sailing to Aberdeen before continuing to Peterhead where she lay overnight. The following day calls were made at Fraserburgh, Banff, Portsoy,

The *St. Magnus* (I) from a large framed print. She was built as the *Waverley* in 1864 for the Silloth - Belfast route of the North British Railway. Three years later she joined the Aberdeen, Leith & Clyde fleet and became both the first vessel to be given a 'Saint' name and their final paddle steamer. (*Author's collection*)

Cullen, Lossiemouth, Findhorn, Nairn, Cromarty, Fortrose and Fort George, arriving at Inverness at 20.30. The return voyage was made in two similar daily passages on the 24th/25th August.

Whichever way the company had intended to operate their two ships, the *Tourist* was withdrawn for refitting at Leith on 7th August 1821 after which she took up the Leith - London service in mid-September. She appears to have operated thus for a further year after which she was sold to

the London & Edinburgh Steam Packet Co. who maintained that service thereafter.

The *Brilliant* probably made a further trip to Inverness the following week after which both companies terminated operations for the season. For many years, services operated during the summer only, from about April to early October. The 'AL&C' always substituted their smacks on the service during the winter months but also kept some of them operating alongside the *Velocity* during the summer to maintain cargo services.

The *Velocity* and the *Brilliant* both re-entered service in April 1822 after having improvements made to their accommodation. Services had been curtailed to two round trips by each vessel per week and the Inverness visits were not attempted that year as possibly the services previously offered had been unduly generous. Dysart had been dropped from the schedules but both ships were billed to make the Aberdeen to Newhaven passage every Friday, one of the few occasions when they were offering a concurrent service.

The 'L&ASY Co.' altered their schedule at the end of May operating their two Aberdeen trips within the period Monday to Thursday and inaugurating a return Newhaven to Dundee service, outwards on Friday and returning on Saturday. The 'AL&C' possibly saw an opportunity here for they re-introduced a three trip weekly schedule for the *Velocity* at the beginning of June which reverted to the the usual two trips in the first week of September. The *Brilliant* came off service in mid-September being chartered by the Government and the *Velocity* was withdrawn in early October.

The succeeding years saw similar schedules operated, the 06.00 start being a regular feature for a considerable period. There were no further experiments as both companies stuck to their twice weekly service between Aberdeen and Newhaven. However, in 1825, both companies attempted territorial expansion, the 'L&ASY Co.' operated a fortnightly Inverness service during July and August and both companies made one trip tp Wick, presumably to test the market.

In February 1826 the *Brilliant* was offered for sale due to the expiry of the agreement between the owning partners. The 'AL&C' stepped in and bought her, probably to forestall any further competition. Since then, until modern times, the company has never experienced any serious major competition. Only the basic service was operated in 1826 while in 1827 the *Brilliant* made two trips to Inverness and one to Wick. The service to Inverness was organised on a permanent basis in 1829 operating weekly during the summer period. Wick still had an occasional steamer but received a permanent service in 1833, but only fortnightly initially and only during the summer. The Wick steamer this year also extended her run to Kirkwall on a permanent basis after having made a test run the previous year.

The company was now operating the three services (Newhaven, Inverness and Wick/Kirkwall) with the two original steamers and the provision of additional tonnage was becoming imperative. In 1836 therefore, the *Sovereign* appeared, at 378 tons more than twice the tonnage of the earlier pair. The *Sovereign* introduced the system of giving the ships names with a monarchial flavour, this nomenclature being employed for 25 years. The year 1836 was a significant year in that the Wick/Kirkwall service became weekly and was also extended to Lerwick, initially on an alternate week basis. After a decade cautiously experimenting in northern waters and gradually increasing services, 1836 marked the year when the origins of today's service pattern can still be discerned. Some 162 years later, today's *St. Sunniva* (III) route; Aberdeen (Sat.); Stromness (Sat./Sun.); Lerwick (Sun./Mon.) and Aberdeen (Tue.) is the direct successor of the 1836 *Sovereign* route; Aberdeen (Fri.); Wick (Sat.); Kirkwall (Sat.); Lerwick (Sun./Mon.); Kirkwall (Tue.); Wick (Tue.); Aberdeen (Tue.). With the discontinuation of Wick and the substitution of Stromness for Kirkwall little has altered, although the *Sovereign* always commenced and terminated her sailings at Newhaven. In 1838 the company obtained the mail contract and have continued to provide mail services ever since.

Eventually, trade also justified keeping the service running in the winter months. This probably commenced in 1838 for the Aberdeen to Newhaven service as an additional vessel, the *Duke of Richmond*, slightly larger than the *Sovereign,* was built that year. Winter services were introduced in 1848 for Inverness, 1850 for Wick and 1858 for the islands. In 1840/41, the Edinburgh terminal had been moved from Newhaven to Granton, about a mile further west.

Services were basically unchanged in the period 1836 to 1859 though there were a number of fleet changes. The *Brilliant* was lost when wrecked on the North Pier at Aberdeen in 1839 and replaced by the three year old *Bonnie Dundee* in 1840. The *Velocity* was sold in 1844 and replaced by the *Queen* (I), built for the company. Fleet strength was maintained at four vessels most of this time but two additional vessels were acquired in 1849. The first was the two year old *Newhaven* from the Brighton & Continental Steam Packet Co., a thinly disguised 'cover' name for the London Brighton & South Coast Railway. Co., who operated a cross-Channel service but she was only retained for a year and a half and sold in 1851. The other vessel was the *Hamburg*, built for the company as their first iron ship, but she was herself sold in 1852. Generally, services could be maintained by three vessels, so a fleet of four was probably adequate to cover overhauls etc. and so an increase to six in the years between 1849 and 1852 appears curious. Could the strangely named *Hamburg* have held a clue to an envisaged further territorial expansion ?

After thirteen years with the company, the *Bonnie Dundee* was sold in 1853, thus reducing the fleet once again to three vessels and it appears that it was in this year that Aberdeen to Granton sailings as a separate service ceased, though of course the northern sailings invariably commenced at Granton, Aberdeen being effectively an intermediate port of call. It is unclear when the intermediate places between Aberdeen and Granton ceased to be ports of call and as the section between Arbroath and Aberdeen was finally rail connected in 1850 they probably fell victim to this new mode of transport at that time. The ports along the Fife coast section were progressively rail connected between 1863 and 1883 but by the early 1850s there were other competing steamboat owners operating in the Firth of Forth and they had probably taken over the local traffic by then. For most, if not all, of the period 1821 to c.1850 the intermediate calling places on the east coast remained as Stonehaven, Montrose, Arbroath, Crail, Anstruther and Elie, although Johnshaven (between Stonehaven and Montrose) was employed from 1824 to c.1831 and possibly later, and Largo (west of Elie) was mentioned in 1853. Dysart may have been dropped at the end of the first (1821) season but is also mentioned in 1853. One other vessel joined the fleet in 1847, the smallest ever owned by the company. This was the tug *Victory* and her main function appears to have been to tender to the other vessels as and when required., She was stationed in Aberdeen and apart from tendering to vessels lying in the harbour she apparently also carried out this function on occasions when 'AL&C' vessels lay off Aberdeen instead of entering, presumably when tidal conditions or commercial considerations so dictated.

From 1850, an additional sailing was provided to Wick and this was extended to Scrabster in 1852. This was the start of the Caithness route, a service which operated for over 100 years and on its introduction it was usual for the Wick call to be dropped from the 'indirect' steamer's itinerary during the winter months. 'Indirect' in this context referred to the Aberdeen-Wick-Kirkwall-Lerwick route as opposed to the 'direct' Aberdeen-Lerwick route which only commenced

The *Queen* (II) at Lerwick. The first screw steamer in the fleet, she entered service in 1861 replacing the wrecked *Duke of Richmond*. (*A H Gilbertson*)

in 1891. This terminology appears to have been introduced in 1966. For virtually all its existence the Caithness steamer left Granton on a Monday or Tuesday, calling at Aberdeen the same day and after making the north calls returning to Granton on Thursday evenings.

The very early steamers were in the 150 to 400 ton range but the *Duke of Richmond* was around 500 tons and the *Hamburg* was almost 700 tons. Apart from the coastal east coast sailings the usual pattern up to 1859 saw departures from Newhaven/Granton on Mondays for Caithness, Tuesdays for Inverness, the usual calling ports (though not necessarily all every trip) being Banff, Cullen, Lossiemouth, Burghead, Cromarty, Invergordon, and Fort George. The Friday sailing was to Wick, Kirkwall and Lerwick and normally all sailings called at Aberdeen in both directions. The Inverness service was terminated in 1859, no doubt due to the fact that Aberdeen and Inverness were rail linked in 1858 but strangely, it was reintroduced in 1874 for one year

11

The *St. Magnus* (I) (ex *Waverley*) at Lerwick. (*A Deayton collection*)

only.

The *Queen* (I) was lost when she struck the Carr Rock off Fife Ness on 19th April 1857 and the *Duke of Richmond* was another loss on 8th October 1859 when she stranded on the Aberdeenshire shore about one and a half miles north of the River Don. To compensate, the new *Prince Consort* joined the fleet in March 1858 while the *Hamburg* was re-purchased from her Grimsby owners in 1860. However, fleet strength

was down to two vessels for much of the period 1857 to 1860 and a number of chartered vessels were employed to assist, this being the first occasion that chartering was recorded. They included the *Commodore*, (1857/8); the *Earl of Aberdeen*, (1857/8); and the *Duke of Rothesay*, (1858). All three came from the Aberdeen Steam Navigation Co. who operated the Aberdeen to London service.

To reinstate the fleet to four vessels the *Queen* (II) was

built in September 1861 and was effectively a replacement for the *Duke of Richmond* which had been lost two years earlier. The *Queen* (II) was noteworthy in that she was the first screw steamer in the fleet. The *Hamburg* was wrecked on Scotston Head in October 1862 and the *Prince Consort* was seriously damaged in May 1863 when she struck the North Pier at Aberdeen. She was sold in that condition, the purchaser reconstructing her and selling her back to the 'AL&C' later the same year. Initially the *Dundee* was chartered from the Dundee, Perth & London Co. to provide cover as this mishap had reduced the fleet to two vessels. Another paddler, the *Vanguard*, was later purchased from the Steam Packet Co. of Dublin to temporarily fill the gap and she brought ship strength up to three initially, and to four once the *Prince Consort* rejoined the fleet. Unfortunately the *Prince Consort* was herself wrecked on the Altens Rock, a couple of miles south of Aberdeen, on 11th May 1867 and as this left the 'AL&C' with only two vessels once again, the *Princess Alice* was chartered from the Aberdeen & Newcastle Shipping Co until a replacement could be found, while the *Dundee* (Dundee, Perth & London Co.) was also on charter during April and May. The second vessel in the fleet, the *Brilliant*, had been lost in 1839. The following two decades were loss free and the 'AL&C' appears to have been more unfortunate than most in that four vessels, the *Queen* (I), the *Duke of Richmond*, the *Hamburg* and the *Prince Consort* had all been lost through marine peril in the decade 1857 to 1867.

The New Dawn

While the geographical extension of services had followed a slow continuous pattern over the years, the links with the outparts and Aberdeen/Leith, with the possible exception of Wick, had invariably been on the basis of a weekly call at best. All this was to change in 1866 when a second vessel was allocated to the 'indirect' route, known as the 'secondary indirect' vessel. The basic schedule was Granton (Tues) - Aberdeen (Wed) - Kirkwall (Wed/Thur) - Lerwick (Thur/Fri) - Kirkwall (Fri) - Aberdeen (Sat) - Leith (Sat). The *Queen* (II) was the first vessel allocated to this route. This service appears to have operated only during the summer, though this was modified after 1937 and was continued in one form or another until 1966. The replacement for the *Prince Consort* was the *Waverley*, the first of that name, and originally built in 1864 for the Silloth-Belfast route of the North British Company. She had been used very little by the 'NB' who felt her to be a poor performer. Early in 1867 she was overhauled and fitted out on the Tyne and entered north service at the end of that year. She was renamed *St. Magnus* (I), commencing a style of nomenclature still in use some 130 years later. She was also noteworthy in that she was the last paddler to join the fleet, and the only two funnel vessel ever owned (until the introduction of the ro-ro vessels). At just over 600 tons, she was of similar size to the *Hamburg*, the *Prince Consort* and the *Vanguard* and was generally employed on the 'indirect' route. Presumably to minimise stress on her paddle wheels, she appears never to have done any winter work in her long career and would normally appear in service between mid-March/mid-April and would then be laid up from about the end of October.

The *Vanguard* was sold in 1868 for breaking up and was replaced the same year by the new *St. Clair* (I), the second screw steamer in the fleet. Although slightly greater in tonnage then the *St. Magnus* (I) she was 20 feet shorter and initially operated the Caithness service, commencing in March of that year.

From 1821 to 1867, some thirteen steamers had joined

Deck saloon of the *St. Magnus* (I), ex *Waverley*. *(Wotherspoon collection)*

The *St. Clair* (I) in original condition. She entered service in 1868. *(Author's collection)*

the 'AL&C' and of them six had been secondhand purchases. Each had averaged nine years with the Company. New vessels in that period had averaged 15 years in company service. The introduction of the *St. Clair* (I) in 1868 must have marked a major turning point in the company's economic circumstances as for the next 45 years, all vessels built for the 'AL&C' arrived new from the builders. It was only the outset of the 1914-18 war that reversed this trend.

The *St. Clair* (I) was followed in 1871 by the *St. Nicholas,* the only time this name was ever used and one of the few occasions when a 'Saint' name has never been repeated. The *St Nicholas* took over the Caithness service and she and the *St. Clair* (I) largely shared the route between them until the turn of the century. These vessels were clipper bowed and were difficult to tell apart, their sterns being their most differentiating feature.

By this time the fleet of four (three 'Saints' plus another) was clearly a 'Saint' line, though this descriptive term appears never to have been employed. The *St. Nicholas* at 787 tons was the largest, the other two Saints being just over the 600 tons, while the *Queen* (I) at 328 tons was the smallest. In addition it was an exceptionally modern fleet in 1871: the *Queen* 10 years, the *St. Magnus* (7 years), the *St. Clair* (3 years), plus the new *St Nicholas*, the average age profile of 5 years never to be attained again.

At this stage if we revert to the actual services we have to recall that for almost the first 50 years of the steamers, many of the services were summer only, though summer in this context extends from the March/April - October period. Inverness was the first to get a winter service in 1848/9, the 'indirect' service to Wick and Kirkwall 1850/51 and the extension to Lerwick (fortnightly at first) was not until

1858/9. It was not until the winter of 1861/2, with the introduction of *Queen* (II), that Lerwick received a weekly winter service which allowed the schooner *Fairy* (which had been the winter Lerwick vessel) to be disposed of. The *Fairy* was the last sailing vessel in the fleet. The Caithness steamer commenced winter service in 1857/8 and in 1861 an extension to Stornoway (Lewis) was introduced. The Stornoway link was unusual in that it was invariably only a seasonal route to handle the herring traffic during the boom years. The frequency was weekly and appears to have been virtually confined to the May/June period.

The Stornoway link was also unique in that the Stornoway-Scrabster section was also served by the steamers of the Hutchison/MacBrayne fleet. This was normally performed by the steamer allocated to the Glasgow-Stornoway route extending her May/June sailings to Scrabster. While this was a very short season, it was highly intensive, shifting thousands of fishworkers (basically all female apart from the buyers, foreman and coopers) eastwards at the beginning of the season and returning them home at the end, though many would follow the migrating fish to the herring stations of Lerwick, Peterhead and Lowestoft/Great Yarmouth.

In June 1875 the Aberdeen, Leith & Clyde Shipping Co. became the North of Scotland, Orkney & Shetland Steam Navigation Co - usually abbreviated to the 'North Co.'

In 1881 it was decided that Shetland would receive a third weekly sailing and this was inaugurated by the *Queen* (II) as a seasonal summer sailing that year. There was one major alteration in that after leaving Aberdeen, she proceeded to Stromness and Scalloway, rather than Kirkwall and Lerwick, thus servicing the western side of the two island groups. Due to the difficulties in road travel in Shetland, this service also called at various west coast ports including Spiggie, Walls, Brae, Voe, Aith and Hillswick, generally fortnightly in summer and monthly in winter. Hillswick, where the company opened their own St. Magnus Hotel in 1900, was served weekly during the summer. Occasional calls were also made at Reawick on Ronas Voe (an important herring fishing station during the season) but these did not appear in the timetables. Orkney was not totally neglected as the southbound steamer normally called at St. Margaret's Hope fortnightly after leaving Stromness.

The Expansionist Decade (1882 - 1892)

From 1836 until 1881, the fleet had always remained at three or four vessels, this sometimes including one or two on charter. The next decade saw fleet size increase to seven by 1887 and nine by 1892. Thereafter it remained at nine or ten until the 1939-45 Second World War. This decade of expansion saw the introduction of a number of new routes and to some extent mirrored the expansion of the Shetland fishing trade.

For about 500 years there has been a ferry crossing between Caithness and Orkney, and it was in 1856 that a locally-owned Stromness vessel commenced a steamer service between Stromness and Scrabster. In 1874 the Highland Railway reached Wick and Thurso. In 1877, having obtained the mail contract, it comenced operating the route, seeing this as a logical extension to their northern main line. When Scapa Pier (2 miles from Kirkwall) was opened in 1880, this became the Orkney terminal, Stromness being relegated to a twice-weekly call. The route was apparently not profitable and the North Company took it over in 1882 building the *St. Olaf* specially for the route. This was the shortest route ever operated by the company and on a daily Monday -Saturday basis. The North Company reinstated

The *St. Margaret* (II) at St Margaret's Hope Pier. (*Author's collection*)

The *St. Rognvald* (I) as built in 1883. She was the AL&C's first ship of over 1,000 gross tons and inaugurated Norwegian fjord cruises in 1886. (*G.Donaldson collection*)

Stromness as the home port and Scapa Pier became a daily call in each direction for the uplift and delivery of mails. Hoxa, a headland near St Margaret's Hope, was a calling place, not always on a daily basis, where passengers were ferried ashore in a small boat.

The *St. Rognvald* (I) joined the fleet in 1883 and at just over 1,000 tons was the largest vessel. She spent most of her career on the main indirect route. However, she was especially noteworthy in that she was the vessel used for the inauguration of the Norwegian cruise programme in 1886, a series of fine ten-day cruises from Leith and Aberdeen, covering the period 24th June to 24th August. This was such a success that the company built the *St. Sunniva* (I) in 1887

specifically for this duty and her appearance was of a large steam yacht which was designated 'S.Y.' on the official company postcards. The *St. Sunniva* was noteworthy in that she was the first purpose-built cruise vessel in the world and the first company vessel to be built with the relatively new triple expansion engine. Thereafter the subsequent steamships built for the company were fitted out with the same engines.

The Norwegian cruising season usually operated from late May until mid-September and encompassed the Norwegian coast and fjords bwteen Stavanger in the south to Trondheim to the north. A steam launch was carried (also on the *St. Rognvald*) to ferry passengers ashore at the various ports of call and on certain shore excursions it allowed passengers to re-embark at a different location from their landing point. Those *St. Sunniva* cruises were so popular that the *St. Rognvald* had to be enlisted to take the overflow for the two July cruises in the first year. Henceforth the *St. Rognvald* was incorporated into the advertised cruising programme every year, apart from in 1890, but her absence from the regular routes. meant that the North Company had to charter tonnage for their own domestic services. The *Ethel* (from MacBraynes) was employed during July/August 1889 and the *Quiraing* (McCallum & Co) from June to August 1891. The summer tonnage shortage was only cured when the *St Giles* (I) joined the fleet in 1892.

There was further expansion in the Norwegian cruising in 1888 when the *St. Sunniva* and the *St. Rognvald* were

rescheduled for the summer season so that their earlier 10-day cruises were extended to 12 days duration and allowed for a regular fortnightly departure from Leith/Aberdeen and weekly when both vessels operated. The *St. Rognvald* had a slightly shorter season thatn the *St. Sunniva*. This eventually stabilised as Saturday departures from Leith/Aberdeen to Stavanger with Tuesday departures from Bergen ten days later for the return voyage. The first sailing for the 1888 season was for a 21-day North Cape cruise undertaken by the *St. Rognvald* and the final sailing advertised for the *St. Sunniva* was for a Baltic cruise which didn't operate. In subsequent years the programme included one cruise to each of these destinations and in 1898 both vessels made a Baltic cruise, the *St. Rognvald* in May/June and the *St. Sunniva* in August/September. An unusual feature of the cruising programme was that passengers could break their journey at any of the ports of call, returning by the following or any subsequent sailing.

Reverting to 1877, a company called the Shetland Islands Steam Navigation Company had been formed to provide a steamer service between Lerwick and the north isles of Shetland with the *Earl of Zetland* (I). 50% of this company appears to have been owned by the North Company and was fully absorbed by them in 1890. This brought another route into the North Company's operations as inter-island sailings continued as before. At 253 tons gross (186 prior to its lengthening in 1884) the *Earl of Zetland* was very much the 'baby' of the fleet, about half the tonnage of the *Queen* (II).

The next and final new route to be introduced to the company's schedules was the 'direct' route from Leith/Aberdeen to Lerwick with no intermediate calls. This was inaugurated by the *St. Nicholas* in the summer of 1891 and was virtually unique to the main services. It operated

The Argyll Steamship Company's *Argyll*, chartered during the 1891-1892 winter for the 'direct' route. (*A . Deayton collection*)

twice weekly departing Aberdeen on Mondays and Thursdays and leaving from Lerwick on Tuesdays and Saturdays, spending the weekends in Leith. During the winter months the route was reduced to one round trip weekly. Perhaps due to the winter overhaul programme the route was covered by the chartered *Argyll* (Argyll Steamship Company) during the first winter. The *St Giles* (I) was built in 1892 and appears to have been used solely for this route during her short career of ten years. At 407 tons gross (later lengthened 23 feet making 465 tons) was the smallest of the main service liners.

The *St. Olaf* also had a very short career on the Pentland Firth from 1882-1890 and, reputedly underpowered, was sold to Canadian interests. For two years a variety of vessels serviced the route with the *John O' Groats* (McCallum & Co), the *Argyll* (Argyll Steamship Co), the *Express* (G. Robertson) and the company's own *Queen* (II) also taking spells of duty. The final vessel during this decade was the *St. Ola* (I) which commenced service on the Pentland Firth route in 1892. It should be noted that *St. Ola* is the Orkney variation of *St. Olaf*, hence the change in the ship's name.

Two ships were converted to triple expansion machinery, the *St. Olaf* in 1890 and the *St. Nicholas* in 1891, but strangely the *St. Rognvald* (I) was not included where fuel savings could have been much greater in her case. By 1892 the nine ships in the fleet included four which were no more than nine years old, although the other five ranged between fifteen and thirty-one years old, giving an average of 15 years overall. The routes operated provided a pattern which was to exist, albeit with some adjustments, until 1956 when the Caithness service ceased, or 1975 if the Shetland north isles routes are taken as the cut-off point. The present ro-ro routes retain recognisable similarities with those other services operated over a century ago.

The *St. Giles* (I), probably at Lerwick. She joined the fleet in 1892 but was lost on Rattray Head in September 1902. (*Author's collection*)

The Consolidation Era (1891 - 1914)

This next period was identified by the North Company withdrawing from the Norwegian cruise trade and replacing older ships with others which were larger and equipped to a higher standard, improving facilities for passengers and providing greater cargo capacity.

The first new vessel was the *St Ninian* (I) in 1895. She had spells on most of the main routes, but she was particularly associated with with the secondary indirect route for most of her lengthy career. She was effectively an able and sound vessel bringing the fleet up to ten ships.

On 24th April 1900, on her usual passage from Lerwick to Kirkwall (main indirect service), the *St. Rognvald* (I) ran

The *St. Ninian* (I) arriving at Aberdeen. Built in 1895, she brought the North Co. fleet up to ten. (*N. McKillop*)

A rare picture of the short-lived *St. Magnus* (II). She was sunk off Peterhead in February 1918. (*John Styring*)

aground in thick fog on Burgh Head, Stronsay. While all the passengers were safely taken off by the lifeboats, all the livestock was lost. Her deckhouse was subsequently salvaged and now serves as a summer house in a Kirkwall garden.

Unlike their northern routes where the company had a near monopoly of services, the Norwegian cruising season had attracted quite a few competitors. Both Currie's Castle Line, and the Union Steamship Company (prior to their 1899 amalgamation) provided a single cruise in 1887. Wilson's of Hull (from 1886) and Salvesen's of Leith (from 1887) provided regular North Sea crossings/cruises and numerous others were attracted to the scene. Presumably this competition played a part in the North Company's decision to restrict their own Norwegian cruises to a single ship operation following the loss of the *St. Rognvald* (I).

After the loss of *St. Rognvald* (I) the *St. Sunniva*'s programme dropped her longer distance cruises to the North Cape and the Baltic apart from a Baltic cruise operated in the 1900 season. The programme now consisted of seven fjord cruises followed by the round Britain cruise lasting about three months at the end of the season. A single fjord cruise in 1902 commenced at Tilbury, apparently the only occasion that this was offered. However, the Norwegian cruising programme was obviously feeling the effects of competition, especially from those companies operating larger ships with better facilities. The Orient Line's *Chinburay* had made a trip from London in 1889 and was joined by the *Garonne* for the July/August season in 1891. In 1907 the North Company only operated six Norwegian cruises while the 1908 season was cut back to two months,

The *St. Nicholas* off Aberdeen. Built in 1871 for the Caithness service, she was the only North Company vessel to receive this name. (*John Styring*)

The *St. Nicholas* aground off Wick, c1902. (*Wick Society*)

although two round Britain cruises were provided that year, the first cruise sailing anti-clockwise - probably the first time ever that had ever occurred. Innovation was not entirely lacking, and in 1901 the *St. Sunniva* provided a round Britain cruise at the end of her Norwegian cruising season proceeding from Leith to Gravesend where the cruise had commenced. This appears to have been repeated every season thereafter. While calls varied from year to year, Torquay, Dartmouth, Plymouth, Isle of Man, Greenock, Oban and Stornoway were usually visited and calls were occasionally made at Dublin, Rothesay and Skye. At least one call was usually made at Stromness, Kirkwall or Lerwick on these cruises, something which rarely occurred on the Norwegian sailings. 1908 saw the end of the Norwegian

cruising programme after 23 years. The *St. Sunniva* (I) was converted to a more conventional mail steamer and took over the direct route between Leith/Aberdeen and Lerwick, rarely deviating from this service.

A replacement, the *St. Rognvald* (II), entered service in 1901 and was the second vessel to exceed the 1,000 ton mark. For her first 24 years she was generally operated on the main indirect service. The *St Giles* (I) was wrecked when she ran aground near Rattray Head lighthouse (between Fraserburgh and Peterhead) in thick fog on 28th September 1902 . She was replaced by the *St Giles* (II) in 1903 which was placed on the direct route. The *St. Magnus* (I) was sold the same year to Gibraltar interests and whatever perceived failings were attributed to her, she was a most competent vessel during her 36 years with the North Company. Following the disposal of the *Vanguard* in 1868, the *St. Magnus* (I) had been the sole paddler in the fleet. Though little used in the winter periods, she appears to have suffered little from paddle wheel failures and had generally operated a 'long' season, approximately March/April to the end of October. This was curtailed by about a month in the early part of the season from the early 1890s, but from 1896/7 she normally provided the twice weekly direct service from July to September. Her final full season was in 1901 when she was replaced by the new *St. Rognvald* (II). Her final two years were essentially as 'spare' vessel, being in operation for about nine weeks in 1902 and only four weeks in 1903. She managed a further ten years on Mediterranean service, running between Gibraltar and Tangier before going to Dutch breakers.

Another innovation for the company was a Mediterranean cruise from London in March 1896, the majority of passengers joining either at Marseilles (on 1st April) or Naples the following day. Lengthy calls were made at Piraeus, Constantinople, Jaffa and Alexandria, returning to Naples on 1st May and Marseilles two days later.

The first purpose-built cruise vessel - the *St. Sunniva* (I) in the Norwegian fjords. *(WSPL)*

The *St. Sunniva* (I). Her cruises ended in 1908 after which she was converted for mail steamer use. *(Author's collection)*

One further vessel remains to be mentioned, the *St Fergus*, built for the company in 1913. This was a small cargo coaster, the first in the fleet, and her intended role in somewhat obscure as she was sold before completion to an Argentinian company.

War and Aftermath (1914 - 1924)

When the First World War commenced, the fleet consisted of eight vessels. The ninth, the *St Nicholas*, had been lost in June of that year. This was adequate in that five vessels could maintain the main routes with one each

The *St. Sunniva* (I), probably off Aberdeen, after conversion for the Lerwick service in 1908. She was lost in April 1930 after grounding on Mousa. All passengers and crew got ashore safely but bad weather prevented the vessel from being salvaged. (*John Styring*)

allocated to the North Isles and the Pentland Firth, allowing one to be spare. However, during the period 1909 to 1914, two ships had been allocated to the direct route during the summer, reducing the service to one in the winter.

Activities during the war are relatively obscure, although the *St. Ninian* (I) served as a naval ferry for most of the conflict, sailing between Scrabster and Scapa Flow. Three ships, the *St. Sunniva* (I), the *St. Magnus* (II) and the *St Margaret* were all chartered out for periods, under the control of G & J Burns Ltd. Perhaps due to this factor, three cargo ships were purchased in 1916, one being the erstwhile *St Fergus* which, at last, sailed under the company's house flag. The *Temaire* was bought from James McKelvie of Glasgow, but only remained with the company for a year

Lerwick pier with the *Earl of Zetland* (I) left, and a large crowd meeting the *St. Sunniva* (I) arriving from Aberdeen. The *St. Magnus* (III) to the rear left. (*Author's collection*)

The *Earl of Zetland* (I) at Lerwick. She was acquired from the Shetland Isles Steam Navigation Co. in 1890. (*Author's collection*)

before being sold again. The third of this trio was the *Cape Wrath* from the Cape Steam Shipping Company of Glasgow.

Three ships were lost during the war, all within a 10 month span. The first was the *Express* which had earlier served on charter on the Pentland Firth for periods between 1890 and 1892. She had been the fourth wartime ship to be purchased in 1917, but was lost in a collision off the French coast in April of that year, achieving the dubious distinction of having the shortest career of any North Company vessel. What she was doing so far from 'home' is unknown, but she could have conceivably been a supply vessel for the British Army in France. On the 12th September 1917 the *St Margaret*, on passage from Lerwick to Iceland, was torpedoed

thirty miles east of the Faroes and sank rapidly with the loss of five of her crew. Her master was Captain William Leask who sailed 150 miles to Shetland in a lifeboat with eighteen of his crew landing at Hillswick after three days. Captain Leask was later in command of the *St. Clair* (I) when she was attacked by a submarine off Fair Isle on 19th January 1918, when two of the crew were killed. The attackers were driven off and Captain Leask received the DSC for this action. The final loss was the *St. Magnus* (II) due to enemy action off Peterhead on 12th February 1918 while on a passage from Lerwick to Aberdeen. Two passengers and one crew member were lost at that time.

The company made a fifth purchase in 1918 when the

The *St. Rognvald* (II) arriving at Leith after World War II She was not broken up until 1951 - her fiftieth year. (*G E Langmuir*)

Cape Wrath was obtained from G & J Burns and renamed the *Ape* though the change in the namestyle has never been explained. She was lost post-war after striking rocks in St. Malo Roads on 13th April 1919, suggesting that her role may have been as a replacement for the *Express*.

At the end of the war the fleet stood at nine, one more than in 1914, but there were some major changes. Three of the fleet were now small cargo coasters and there were only four main line service vessels, the youngest, *St. Rognvald*, being 17 years old and with the average age of this quartet being 30 years. With the loss of their two newest vessels, the average age of the fleet was 26 years, five years more than when the conflict started.

The conditions in the post-war depression years meant that there was no new-build programme. The loss of the *Fetlar* (I) was made good by the purchase of the 36 year old *Cavalier* from MacBraynes in 1919, which was renamed the *Fetlar* (II). She only remained in the fleet for a year and spent part of her service on the north isles route. A second purchase from MacBraynes, also in 1919, was their *Chieftain* which was renamed the *St Margaret* (II) and was employed on the west side service. Passenger services were curtailed immediately after the war mainly because the *St Ninian* did not reappear from her post-war reconditioning until the winter of 1919. The 1919 summer programme consisted only of the direct (once weekly), the main indirect and west side services. There was no secondary indirect service or Caithness steamer. Services were nearer normality in 1920, but the *St. Sunniva*, although reverting to twice weekly service between Aberdeen and Lerwick, did not call at Leith. This may have been due to the inflationary cost of coal and and numerous strikes at this period, or to the shortage of experienced officers. The Caithness service was not fully restored until the 1921 season.

The *St. Ola* (I) departing from Stromness. The steamer enjoyed a remarkable 59 year career (1892-1951) on the Pentland Firth. (*Author's collection*)

From 1921 the allocation of main line service vessels was:

Direct	*St. Sunniva* (I)
Main Direct	*St. Rognvald* (II)
Secondary	*St Ninian* (I)
West side	*St Margaret* (II)
Caithness	*St. Clair* (II)

The *St. Ola* and the *Earl of Zetland* operated on the minor routes with the *Cape Wrath* and *St Fergus* looking after cargo commitments. As the secondary indirect route was a summer only service, there was always a spare vessel to cover winter overhauls.

Landing at Hoxa from the *St. Ola* (I) in Androo's Boat. The flit-boat was the usual method of disembarkation at the islands without suitable piers. (*Author's collection*)

Farewell to Orkney. A common postcard: loading a cow onto the *St. Rognvald* (II). (*Author's collection*)

Between the Wars (1924 - 1939)

The economic climate had been improving during the early part of the 1920s as the *St. Magnus* (III) joined the fleet in 1924, the first new-build ship since the two in 1912/13. She replaced the *St Margaret* (II) which was sold to Canada in 1925 after only six years in the fleet and had a long and honourable career in British Columbia until 1945. The arrival of the *St. Magnus* (III) marked a considerable increase in the size of the main line vessels. Apart from the two *St. Giles'*, virtually all the main line steamers from 1868 had been between 700 and 1,100 tons gross. The *St. Magnus* (III) was relatively massive at almost 1,600 tons gross and

with considerable passenger accommodation, originally 234 berths in the First Class and 84 in the Second Class, a combined total which was not to be exceeded until the introduction of the ro-ro ferries some 50 years later. While many of the cabins were 2/4 or 4-berth, the original configuration included two 16-berth cabins and one 8/18-berth cabin which was in the First Class area! Strangely there were no 2-berth cabins and Second Class passengers were restricted to two 42-berth cabins. The three main public rooms in the First Class section were also adaptable in that the settee seating around the sides was convertible to an upper and lower bunk configuration and by this means it added 16 berthed passengers in the smoking room, 16 in the winter dining saloon and 24 in the summer dining saloon helping to accommodate the peak of extra summer passengers. The *St. Magnus* (III) also broke new ground in that she had three hatches and corresponding holds, Numbers 1 and 2 forward, and Number 3 aft. Previous vessels had been provided with single holds fore and aft. These were worked by three steam cranes, all as was customary, mounted on to the starboard side of the ship. The impression of size was further enhanced by the three deck bridge structure, an innovation giving the wheelhouse etc., officers' accommodation and the smoking room (lounge). In all previous vessels the smoking room, where provided, had been sited at the aft deck house. On the introduction of the *St. Magnus* (III) she was placed on the main indirect route, displacing the *St. Rognvald* (II) to the west side route.

Four years later (1928) the *St. Clement* (I) joined the fleet, replacing the *Cape Wrath* after eleven years of service.

The *St. Catherine* (I) (ex *Lairdsbank*, ex *Olive*) probably approaching Scalloway during summer 1930. (*Williamson, Scalloway - John Styring*)

Stern view of the *St. Rognvald* (II) with a yellow funnel. (*R J Scott*)

The *St. Clement* (I) was another cargo ship but also innovatory in that she had limited passenger accommodation for twelve in the mid-ship accommodation block. Her main duty was as winter Caithness steamer from approximately mid-October to May, although in the late 1930s she was terminating about a month earlier. Her other main duty was to relieve the *Earl of Zetland* (I) for approximately 3-4 weeks generally during late September-early October, and it is believed that she had a limited passenger certificate for this duty. During early September she normally spent 2-3 weeks as a seasonal livestock carrier, shipping sheep and cattle from the islands to Aberdeen. For the remainder of the summer she varied her activities between coping with 'overflows' on the main routes and acting as a general tramping coaster, frequently loading coal cargoes from

27

The beautiful *St. Sunniva* (II) off Aberdeen, probably on builder's trials in 1931. (*John Styring*)

mistaken for a large steam yacht, although the two steam cranes betrayed her true role as a coastal passenger steamer. Although dimensionally slightly larger than the *St. Magnus* (III), her smaller superstructure was largely responsible for her tonnage being about 200 gross, less than her immediate predecessor. She had one hundred and twelve First Class berths, less than half the capacity of the *St. Magnus* (III), of which ten were 2-berth cabins. There were fourteen 2/4-berth cabins and a ladies cabin sleeping sixteen. The dining room sat fifty-four and there was a smoking room in the aft

29

The St. Magnus (III) off Lerwick. The steamer joined the fleet in 1924 and remained in service until 1960. (Author's collection)

deck house. The Second Class gents cabin was able to sleep fifty-four in berths, probably the largest number ever provided for, and in addition there were settees which could have accommodated a further sixteen to eighteen. The ladies cabin had berths for eighteen plus settees for four or five.

One peculiarity was that the only access to the ladies cabin was by negotiating the gents cabin!

The *St. Sunniva* (II) was placed on the direct route on which she served for virtually all her peace-time service. The *St. Magnus* (III) and *St. Rognvald* (II) reverted to the main indirect and the west side routes respectively and while the *St. Catherine* (I) was retained, she became virtually the excess vessel. From her introduction, the *St. Magnus* (III) was originally a summer-only ship (June to September) but did serve on her own route during the winters of 1935/6 and 1936/7 and on the direct routes during the winters of 1937/8 and 1938/9. The *St. Sunniva* (II) also became a summer only boat, although her four month duty extended to about six months from the 1937 season onwards. The winter service on the direct route became a regular duty for the *St Catherine* (I) and there was the unusual arrangement whereby the direct route had two vessels allocated to it - a summer boat and a winter boat. The *St Catherine* (I) made occasional appearances on the west side route outwith her normal winter duty and also relieved the main indirect service at times. In July/August 1933 she had a short charter to the Aberdeen, Newcastle & Hull Steam Company but otherwise the summers were idle at the lay-up buoys in the Victoria Dock, Aberdeen.

The *St. Clair* (I) finished her season on the Caithness

The *St. Colm* (ex *St Clair* (I)) at Leith on 28th April 1937, her final season in service. (*Author's collection*)

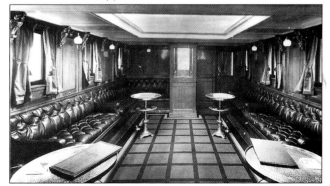

The Saloon of the *St. Sunniva* (II). (*Author's collection*)

route on Friday 30th October 1936 for a winter lay-up and in December was renamed the *St. Colm*, the first and only time this name was ever used. This was to release the name for a new-build, the *St. Clair* (II), another innovatory ship. She was the first vessel to have a fully midship superstructure, all earlier vessels having deck houses erected on the shelter deck. The biggest change internally was that First Class accommodation was still amidships and Second Class was aft. The only accommodation forward was for deck and engine crew. Dimensionally and in tonnage she was marginally bigger than the *St. Magnus* (III).

The internal layout of the new *St. Clair* (II) was that the dining saloon, which always appears to have been described on the deck plans of earlier vessels as 'saloon' or 'dining saloon' was now described as the 'restaurant'. Old habits die hard and it's doubtful if stewards or passengers ever used this new terminology. The saloon was a deck higher then on

The *St. Sunniva* (II) at Aberdeen. *(Aberdeen Maritime Museum)*

earlier vessels on the shelter or upper deck at the fore end of the superstructure with numerous windows providing good views of the passing scene. Seating was for 56 in tables for two, four or eight. Above, on the boat deck, was the lounge and this was encircled on three sides by an observation saloon. Aft on the boat deck was a small bar. On earlier vessels the 'bar' had been a small room which was actually a dispensing compartment. Aft of the saloon and on the deck below were the thirty-six cabins, all 2/4-berth convertibles, making provision for 144 berthed passengers. In the Second Class, the smoking room was at the after end of the aft deck house, while the far end had two 4-berth and two 6-berth cabins, somewhat unusually in connected pairs so that a 4-berth had to be negotiated to enter a 6-berth. The entrance lounge with four setees separated cabins from the smoking room. On the main deck below there were four 4-berth and five 6-berth cabins, also a small dining saloon to seat 14, the first time this had been provided in the Second Class area. This was the first ship where 'overflow' bunks were not provided in First Class public rooms, but it was possible to set up a further ten bunks each in the Second Class smoke room and dining saloon. This gave a total of 86 berths in Second Class.

The *St. Clair* (II) spent her first month in service (May 1937) on the main indirect route, but subsequently transferred to the west-side route which she served for the three summers prior to the outbreak of World War II, though winters were spent on the main indirect route.

On the introduction of the *St. Clair* (II) into service, the 44-year-old *St Catherine* (I) was despatched to the breakers in the middle of May 1937. This was followed by the 69-year-old *St. Colm* at the end of July 1937. Even with the disposal of these two elderly vessels, the remaining nine-strong fleet still included four vessels of between thirty-six

and sixty-years-old. It seems possible that with this age profile, the company was considering a rolling programme of replacements, but in the event only one further vessel was ordered and delivered prior to the outbreak of war.

The introduction of the *Earl of Zetland* (II) in August 1939 was as a replacement for her 62-year-old namesake which had been renamed *Earl of Zetland II* - the first occasion this 'II' suffix had been employed by the company. The new *Earl of Zetland* was truly a liner in miniature and was the first diesel-engined vessel in the fleet. All subsequent vessels were similarly engined. On her introduction to service on the North Isles route, her predecessor was laid up in Aberdeen, her future uncertain.

The Second World War (1939 - 1945)

The 1939 war can be considered to have arrived in 1938 for the North Company. As early as September that year the *St.Clement* (I) is recorded as having made three trips for naval military purposes: (1) Aberdeen to Flotta with a gun pedestal; (2) Leith to Lyness with (telegraph) poles and motor cars; and (3) Rosyth to Lyness with Admiralty mooring gear. Lyness was the main naval shore base on the island of Hoy for Scapa Flow and Flotta which was the largest adjacent island, both being of great importance once the conflict started.

Most succeeding months saw the *St. Clement* (I) and the *St Fergus* similarly employed, generally to Lyness, although Longhope, a few miles from Lyness, also featured. Where it has been recorded, cargoes were listed as machinery, huts, motors, tipping wagons, rails, railway sleepers, iron, and in one case, a special charter. The *St. Ninian* (I) also got in the act with five trips divided between Lyness and Longhope. Two special sailings were made in August 1939 for Scottish

Command (the Army), which were probably Territorials' movements. The first was by the *St. Clair* (II), Leith-Lyness-Leith, which she managed to fit into her normal lie-over refit at Leith. A fortnight later the *St. Ninian* (I) operated Leith-Lyness-Scapa (Pier) before reverting to her normal Caithness route. The Lyness traffic had obviously been increasing and in that month the *Naviedale* was chartered to make three Leith-Lyness sailings. In addition, the *St. Rognvald* (II) terminated one of her southbound July sailings in Aberdeen and returned to Kirkwall to bring a contingent of territorials south for their annual camp, travelling direct to Leith.

Although the war commenced on 3rd September 1939, the company had been monitoring the situation for a few weeks beforehand and there had been an exodus of holidaymakers and visitors from the Islands. The first real disruption to normal schedules came when the *St. Sunniva* (II) terminated her service at Leith on 27th Augus and, returned to Aberdeen two days later when she was handed over to the Admiralty. She was followed by the *St. Magnus* (III) which had arrived in Leith on the 30th, returned to Aberdeen and was handed over to the Admiralty on the following day. In addition, the *St. Clair* (II) had not proceeded beyond Scalloway on her sailing from Leith on the 27th, but otherwise provided her normal weekly schedule for that week. The *Earl of Zetland* (II) was reactivated after only eight days of idleness to make a cargo run from Aberdeen to Kirkwall on 30th August, and thereafter proceeded to Scrabster to assist the *St. Ola* (I) on the Pentland Firth route which was about to begin the busiest ever period in its history. The withdrawal of two of the main line fleet units necessitated the rescheduling of the remaining vessels and initially the *St. Ninian* (I) took the rescheduled 28th August sailing from Leith in place of the *St. Sunniva* (II) but her

The *Highlander* at the buoys, Victoria Dock, Aberdeen. She was renamed *St. Catherine* (II) but was sunk by enemy action in November 1940. (*G.R. Scott*)

next sailing, from Aberdeen on 1st September, was on the main indirect service but this was terminated at Lerwick. She then proceeded direct to Scrabster, arriving on 4th September and was handed over to the Admiralty to become the naval ferry for the Pentland Firth service. The withdrawn *Earl of Zetland II*, after only a few days on the Firth, returned to Aberdeen on the same day. By the second day of the war, three of the main line fleet had been requisitioned, leaving only the *St. Clair* (II) and the *St. Rognvald* (II) to cope. The *Earl of Zetland II* was retained until 2nd October taking cargoes from Aberdeen to Wick, Stromness and Kirkwall, but was then laid up until the 26th November, her very limited capacity making her unsuitable, even under the

The *St. Rognvald* (II) at Stromness. (*Author's collection*)

circumstances of the time. The *Naviedale*, joined by the *Rimsdale*, were kept on charter throughout September and October 1939 covering the Caithness route at times, and appearing elsewhere as cargo requirements dictated.

As in the First World War, the purchase of secondhand tonnage was restarted to make up fleet numbers and the first of these was the *Highlander*, a passenger cargo vessel, purchased at the beginning of October 1939 from the Aberdeen, Newcastle and Hull Steam Co., a vessel roughly comparable to the *St. Magnus* (III) and which had been laid up at the outbreak of war. A further purchase was the cargo ship *Rora Head* from A.F. Henry & McGregor of Leith at the beginning of December 1939 and somewhat similar to the *St. Clement* (I). Early in 1940 a third purchase was the small coasting steamer *Amelia* (built 1894) and at 357 tons gross was even smaller than the *St. Fergus*. This purchase was of a rather different nature in that she had been owned by Cooper and Company of Kirkwall since 1920, operating a direct Kirkwall to Leith service and the purchase was effectively a takeover of Coopers, and to the end of her days Coopers retained their own berths, offices and facilities at Leith and Kirkwall. The *Amelia* remained, with few deviations, on her 'own' route virtually to the end of her days. Some further alleviation of the tonnage difficulties resulted when the Caithness route was withdrawn, the final sailing was undertaken by the *St. Fergus* from Leith on 5th April 1940. This was followed by the withdrawal of Scalloway calls as from the Leith sailing on 5th May 1940. The west side service thereafter proceeded no further than Stromness, though it retained the St Margaret's Hope calls. The *St. Fergus* was also the vessel used when the Scalloway calls were terminated.

During 1939 the attempt was made to continue with the long-standing indirect service, but on five different weeks

The cargo steamer *Rora Head* was purchased in 1939 and remained in the fleet until 1956. (*Author's collection*)

The *Earl of Zetland* (II) of 1939 was the North Company's first diesel-powered ship. (*Author's collection*)

there was no vessel available. The problem was further confounded in that the round trip was taking on average 8/10 days so that, it was unusual to find the same vessel making consecutive sailings. Most sailings employed the *St. Rognvald* (II) or the *St. Clair* (III), but the *Highlander* made two trips. The *St. Ninian* (I) and the *St. Clement* (I) also made one sailing each. There were only four sailings in January and February 1940 and one took 16 days for the round journey from Leith. This was followed by a nine week gap covering March and April. May was unusual in that five sailings were made, thereafter there were only isolated sailings for the rest of the year. As earlier, Leith - Lerwick Direct (June - September 1940), Aberdeen to Lerwick (June - September 1940) Leith to Kirkwall (June to November 1940), Aberdeen to Kirwall (June to November 1940) sailings were provided by *St. Rognvald* (II), *Highlander* and

The *St. Clair* (II) leaving Leith on her maiden voyage on 29th April 1937. (*W. Barrie*)

St. Clement (I). Folllowing her de-requisition by the Admiralty, the *St. Magnus* (III) appeared on her old route with a sailing from Leith on 14th August 1940 but this was followed by a ten week gap. There were only a further few isolated sailings all provided by *St. Magnus* (III), the last being on 11th January 1941, after which this service did not resume until 1945.

From November 1940 a major change was that all main services were restricted to a link between two ports and from this date there were separate Leith-Kirkwall and Aberdeen-

Kirkwall services. The Lerwick direct service was initially continued with the same vessel, generally loading at both Leith and Aberdeen, and while a twice weekly schedule could not be maintained, the gaps rarely exceeded a week. Initially sailings were divided between the *St. Rognvald* (II) and the *Highlander,* the latter vessel being replaced by the *St. Magnus* (III) from August 1940. Apart from this, the main services were separated into Leith/Aberdeen to Lerwick and Leith/Aberdeen to Kirkwall sailings, the first of these being effectively a continuation of the direct route. Initially an attempt was made to operate the Kirkwall route twice weekly and until the beginning of October the *St. Clement* (I) made half the sailings, the rest being shared between the *Earl of Zetland II*, the *Naviedale*, the *Rimsdale* and the *Highlander*. There was a three week gap after this, and subsequently, sailings were made at about 5/6 days intervals on average, but the intervals tended to be erratic in duration. Following the October 'gap' and until mid-August 1940, the bulk of the sailings were operated by the *St. Clair* (II),the *St. Clement* (I) and the *Rora Head*, a few by the *St. Fergus* and only isolated appearances by the *St. Rognvald* (II), the *Highlander,* the *Naviedale,* the *Berriedale* (another charter) and the *St. Magnus* (III). The *Highlander* had been attacked by enemy bombers 10 miles south-east of Aberdeen on 2nd August after leaving Aberdeen while operating the Lerwick to Leith sailings. Managing to shoot down two of them, a part of the wreckage of one was strewn across the afterdeck when it crashed. For this action, Captain William Gifford received an OBE, two crew members received the MBE and three others, including stewardess Miss Cockburn, were commended. After three weeks repairing damage at Leith she resumed service, but it was thought prudent to change her name and she thus became the *St. Catherine* (II). From late August 1940 the Kirkwall service continued as before, the *St.*

Catherine (II) taking half the sailings, the others being shared between the *Rora Head*, the *St.Clement* and the *St. Fergus*. It was while thus employed that the *St. Catherine* (II) (formerly *Highlander*)was attacked once again after leaving Aberdeen on 14th November for Kirkwall. Fate was against her on this occasion and she sunk rapidly with the loss of Captain J.G. Norquoy, thirteen crew (including seven from the engine room) and one passenger after a career of just 13 months with the company.

Initially the Lerwick service during 1939 was attempted as a twice weekly sailing but this was difficult to maintain, October having a particularly poor service with no sailings after the 2nd until the 31st. Most sailings were provided by the *St. Rognvald* (II) the *St. Clair* (III) and the *Highlander* with the *St. Ninian* (I),the *St. Clement* (I) and the *St. Fergus* all making appearances. From January 1940 the service tended to be approximately weekly with the *St. Rognvald* (II) and the *Highlander* generally alternating until July, the latter vessel being replaced by the *St. Magnus* (III) thereafter. Two 'strangers' appeared, the *Kildrummy* (possibly a charter) for one trip in August and, from May 1941, the *Blyth* (allotted by Ministry of War Transport) which joined the *St. Rognvald* (II) and the *St. Magnus* (III) until August 1941 when the joint Leith/Aberdeen sailings terminated.

The *Earl of Zetland II* (which had been laid up in Aberdeen) was reactivated again after 2nd October 1939 and returned as second vessel for the Pentland Firth route, this occupying her until 22nd January 1941. She then returned to her old haunts, the north isles of Shetland, for the duration of the war and was normally relieved by the *Earl Sigurd* from Orkney. The new *Earl of Zetland* was requisitioned by Scottish Command and used initially for troop movements from Scrabster and within Scapa Flow. Military control was exercised from Stromness and for the first two months she was a regular visitor to Scapa (Pier), Lyness and less frequently to Longhope and Flotta. Overnight lie-overs were shared between Scrabster and Stromness but occasionally Scapa and St. Margaret's Hope was used. From April 1941 she fell into a fairly regular pattern of leaving Scrabster around 12.00, crossing over to Stromness, often with a call at one of the Scapa Flow ports, and then returning similarly to Scrabster, arriving about 17.00/18.00. From about September the Scrabster departure was brought forward to 09.00/10.00, returning around 15.00/16.00. Scrabster was very much her home port during the war but the Saturday sailing was generally northbound only, providing the weekends at Stromness and resuming service from there on Mondays. The naval ferry, the *St Ninian* (I) was based at HMS *Dunluce Castle*, moored at Scapa Flow making a return crossing daily from there to Scrabster. She was joined by the *Morialta*, a new ship from the Caledon yard for Australian owners but requistioned by the Admiralty and apparently managed by the North Company from October 1940.

For the rest of the war four ships were required to operate the Pentland Firth routes while the *St. Ola* (I) on the commercial service was normally relieved by the *Earl of Zetland* which, operating as a millitary ferry, was relieved by the *St. Ninian* (I). The naval ferry continued as a two ship operation until June 1945 and when the *Morialta* terminated her service at the end of August 1943, she was replaced by the Faroese steamer the *Tjaldar* which had entered the service from June 1943 and was also managed by the North Company. In all, some twenty-one vessels made appearances on the Pentland Firth routes, some for only very short periods. There was some interchange between duties apart from the using relieving arrangements. Both the 'Earls' and the Great Western Railway's Plymouth tender the *Sir*

The *Earl of Zetland* (II) at Lerwick on 19th August 1939, the old *Earl of Zetland* (I) and the *St. Magnus* can also seen in the picture. *(Author's collection)*

Richard Grenville had the distinction of serving on commercial, naval and miltary services. Other vessels which has significant spells on the Pentland Firth were the *Calshot* (Southampton tender) and the escaped Norwegian coastal steamer *Galtesund*, while another Plymouth tender, the *Sir John Hawkins*, appeared on the military service at times.

We return now to September 1939 where the *St. Sunniva* (II) and *St. Magnus* (III) lay at Aberdeen under Admiralty requistion. Both sailed from there on 8th October, the *St. Sunniva* (II) to be an accommodation ship in Scapa Flow and the *St. Magnus* (III) to Kirkwall Bay where she became a guardship for contraband control. Both were briefly diverted in April 1940 for a troopship voyage from Aberdeen to

Norway, the third ship in the convoy being Bank Lines *Cedarbank* which was torpedoed and sunk off the Norwegian coast. The *St. Magnus* (III) had a number of other diversions from her static role in Kirkwall Bay and on some of these her place on duty was taken by the *St. Sunniva* (II). On 15th May 1940 the *St. Magnus* (III) made a voyage from Kirkwall Bay to Lerwick with a contingent of Royal Air Force units, returning on the following day. She departed again on 1st June 1940 and the evidence suggests that she went to Scapa Flow, berthing alongside at Lyness, where embarkation (presumably naval personnel) took place that afternoon. She sailed on the 3rd June arriving at Rosyth the following afternoon where her 'passengers' disembarked. She left Rosyth on 8th June probably for Scapa/Kirkwall where 43 officers and 305 other ranks of army personnel had embarked. the *St. Magnus* (III) sailed around 13.00 on 16th June, arriving at Aberdeen at 05.00 the following morning where the troops disembarked, She returned to Kirkwall Bay from Aberdeen on 13th June.

War losses were the *St. Fergus*, following a collision and the *St. Catherine* (II) by bombing, both in 1940, The *St Clement* (I) was lost by bombing in 1941. The *St. Sunniva* (II) foundered without trace off Newfoundland in January 1943 with the loss of 64 crew.

Reconstruction (1945 - 1951)

At the end of the war (Europe 7th May and Japan 14th August 1945) North Company services were still essentially on a wartime footing, although the *St. Clair* (II) had been handed back to the company at Aberdeen on 19th June for refitting. There were still four allocated ships in the fleet (the *Blyth* and three General Steam Navigation Co. vessels) serving traditional ports. In addition a further two vessels had

The *St. Clair* (II) arriving at Aberdeen in a storm on 20th November 1950. (*Press & Journal*)

been allocated on 16th December 1944 as military transports. There were the *Nova* (Bergen Steamship Company) normally operating Aberdeen-Faroe (until September 1945) and the *Lochnagar* (Aberdeen Steam Navigation Company Ltd) normally operating Aberdeen-Lerwick (until February 1946). Owned vessels on their regular services were the *St. Magnus* (III), *St. Rognvald* (II), *Rora Head*, *Dunleary*, *St. Ola* (II) and the *Earl of Zetland II*.

The *St. Ninian* (I) and the *Earl of Zetland* remained as naval and military ferries on the Pentland Firth.

There was a general derequisition of all allocated vessels effective as from 2nd March 1946 once voyages were completed and the last of the 'outside' fleet departed on 26th March. However, with a severely depleted working fleet, the

The *St. Clair* (II) on trials during 1937. Converted to oil burning in 1946, the ship was renamed *St. Magnus* (IV) in 1960. (*Author's collection*)

Edina was taken on commercial charter (March - June 1946) as was the *Naviedale* (April to June 1946). On the release of the *Earl of Zetland* from military duties, she returned to the North Isles route (December 1945 to March 1946), but was then transferred initially to the Aberdeen-Kirkwall service which had reverted to a twice weekly passenger service before finally returning to her 'own' route. Her predecessor, the 'old Earl' was reallocated to the Pentland Firth for general assisting duties from December 1946 to early March 1947, followed by a final stint on the north isles service until June 1947 when she returned to Aberdeen to lay-up. The *Earl of Zetland II* was sold in October of that year and left Aberdeen on 5th December 1946 for a new life in the Mediterranean.

For the period June 1945 to June 1946 there was an interim phase during which the Aberdeen-Kirkwall and Aberdeen-Lerwick services were provided on a twice weekly basis. The Kirkwall route was provided by the *St. Rognvald* (II), or the *Earl of Zetland* (March to May) leaving Aberdeen on Tuesdays and Fridays and Kirkwall on Mondays and Wednesdays while Lerwick was served by the *St. Magnus* (III), or *St. Rognvald* (II) (April to May), leaving Aberdeen on Mondays and Thursdays and Lerwick on Tuesdays and Saturdays. After a full year refitting and converting, which included conversion to oil burning, for her peace-time role the *St. Clair* (II) took up the twice weekly Lerwick service on 17th June 1946 and thereafter the 'direct' route but did not include a Leith call.

The Indirect service resumed in July 1945 though there was one major difference. The main sailing was now one at the beginning of the week, normally Monday from Leith, while the secondary sailing left Leith on the Thursday. Initially the main sailing was operated by the *Blyth* or the *Aire* (September to November) but calls were not made at Aberdeen in either direction. This service terminated again in mid-December but resumed with the *St. Magnus* (III) in June 1946 on the traditional pattern of calling at Aberdeen both northbound and southbound. The most pressing problem for the company was the purchase of new tonnage and on 26th September 1946 the new *St. Clement* (II) made her maiden voyage from Aberdeen to Kirkwall. She replaced the *Dunleary* which had been sold the previous month to Greek buyers. Like her earlier namesake she was a cargo ship but included some features not provided for on earlier vessels. While her predecessor had been provided with a saloon for the statutory twelve passengers, the new ship was fitted with 2-berth cabins for this number, while the Master had the novelty of both a day room and a bedroom. One of

The 1894-built *Amelia* at Leith in the early fifties. (*G.H. Somner*)

the main duties envisaged for the *St. Clement* (II) was the carriage of livestock and she incorporated a ramped walkway from the upper (shelter) deck, accessible from the starboard side down to the main deck, so that livestock did not require to be lifted by crane off and on. There was also a portable walkway from the main deck down to the lower hold and during the major livestock movements this was regularly left in place. The *St. Clement* (II) fell into a fairly regular pattern during her early years of livestock sailings (September - November), secondary indirect service (November - May), and North Isles (March-April). At other times she effectively acted to clear backlogs or for supplementary sailings. The secondary indirect service had recommenced in September 1945 and notionally was

The *St. Ninian* (II) entered service in 1950 and was sold for further trading in 1971. (*Author's collection*)

The *St. Ola* (II) at Stromness. She maintained the Pentland Firth crossing between 1951 and 1974. (*Author's collection*)

operated fortnightly by the chartered *Edina,* but the service lapsed during March-May 1946. Like the main service, no Aberdeen calls were made in either direction. It reverted to something approaching its pre-war appearance from June 1946 when the *St. Rognvald* was allocated to the Thursday sailing from Leith. The main difference now was that the service terminated at Kirkwall all year round.

The west side service, effectively the Stromness boat with fortnightly calls at St. Margaret's Hope, was covered by the *Rora Head* although the *St. Clement* (II) was employed for periods during late summer and autumn. the *Naviedale* on charter was also used. The *St. Ninian* (I) was finally derequisitioned at Aberdeen in December 1946 and lay there unused for about two years before going to the breakers in 1948 at 53 years of age. Perhaps the most unusual feature of these immediate post-war years was that the *St. Rognvald* was used to relieve the Pentland Firth and the North Isles services during April/May 1947. Perhaps surprisingly it was not until 1950 before a main line vessel was built, though obviously the years of austerity and inflation in the immediate post-war period may have been the reason. The new vessel was the *St. Ninian* (II) and was innovatory in that she was the first twin-screw vessel in the fleet, indeed the only one until the car ferries appeared 26 years later. She also introduced a rather different profile with only one hold forward and two aft. At 2,200 tons there was more scope in distributing the accommodation even though it was all concentrated in the mid-ships area. First Class cabins, mainly 2-berth with some 4-berth, were spread over four decks and, for the first time the decks were identified A (prom deck), B (shelter deck), C (main or upper deck) and D (lower deck). Second Class cabins (4-berth and 6-berth) were situated on C and D decks. The second Class dining room and the lounge/bar were located at the fore end of the accommodation block on B deck and the First Class dining saloon, seating 60, was located directly above. This was rather a high location for such a public room and during mealtimes caused continual difficulties in service in adverse weather conditions. As in the earlier *St. Clair* (II), there was an enclosed observation shelter surrounding the saloon on three sides and in the first year it had to serve as an overflow dining saloon during the peak season. It could seat a further 40 (later increased to 50) and meal service was only possible in that there were two communicating doors between the dining saloon and the observation area. There were very few cabins on A deck and the after end of this section was

divided to form separate lounge and bar areas. The crew were located aft, the first time this had been done, although stewards were mainly on C deck (port side).

On the introduction into service of the *St. Ninian* (II) in June 1950 she was allocated to the main indirect route, displacing the *St. Magnus* (III) to the secondary sailings which now, as in pre-war years, was extended to Lerwick during the June-Sept period. The *St. Rognvald* operated the Stromness service that summer. 1950 was the only post-war year that the Company operated four main line vessels, still one less than in 1939. The *St. Rognvald* finished service in October 1950 and after being laid-up for a few months was sold to breakers. The *St. Ninian* (II) was thus effectively a replacement ship for the *St. Rognvald*.

The other improvement to services that summer was the re-establishment of the Caithness route and the *Rora Head*, being effectively surplus, was available to cover this sector. One change was that Wick was the only Caithness route call until the end of October when Kirkwall was also included. From November the Caithness and Stromness services were generally operated jointly outwith the summer period.

In 1951, the final ship in the post-war reconstruction programme was built. This was the *St. Ola* (II) to replace her elderly 59-year-old namesake. She commenced service at the end of May 1951, her predecessor going to the breakers. In appearance she was an enlarged *Earl of Zetland* but had no well deck forward. With twin lifeboats on each side, she was easily distinguishable from the 'Earl.' Internally the shelter deck had a large, rather spartan deck shelter on the fore end and while the after end was given over to a large well-furnished lounge/bar. The dining saloon was below this on the main deck and six 2-berth passenger cabins were located on the starboard side. There were also two rest rooms on the lower deck, male and female, furnished with settees and a

45

comfortable area where passengers could lie down on a bad day on the Firth. The *St. Ola* (II) was also an innovatory vessel in that she was the first Single Class ship (cargo vessels excluded) in the fleet.

At the end of the war in 1945, the fleet consisted of ten vessels including the two time-expired veterans (the *Earl of Zetland II* and *St. Ninian* (I)) with an average age of 37 years, four of the fleet being in excess of 50! At the end of this reconstruction programme six years later, the eight-strong fleet now averaged 15 years, although this still included the 57-year-old veteran *Amelia*.

The Post-War Period 1951-1974

This quarter century can perhaps be defined as a period of stability with no major changes, although the 'Steam Navigation' became the North of Scotland, Orkney & Shetland Shipping Co. Ltd. in 1953. Only three ships joined the fleet, one being secondhand, but four departed. It can be divided into two separate periods. From 1951 to 1966 services still largely followed the traditional pattern and with considerable resources devoted to expanding the all inclusive cruise and hotel holiday concept. The period from 1967 to 1974 was one of contraction, other than on the freight side, when the main line fleet diminished to only one vessel and all services from Leith ceased.

In 1900 the company had built the St. Magnus Hotel in Hillswick, Shetland, a 4-month seasonal establishment which until 1939 had formed an essential 7-day stop-over link in the 12-day holiday packages from Leith/Aberdeen employing the services of the west side steamer. The 1939 cost was £12 (Leith), £11.50 (Aberdeen). This particular 12-day holiday resumed in 1946 but as there was no longer a Hillswick vessel the 'cruise' part was in the care of the *St.*

Magnus (III) or *St. Ninian* (II) from 1950 and passengers were taken by coach from Lerwick to Hillswick. In 1947 the Standing Stones Hotel at Stenness, Orkney was purchased, which was open all the year round, and tourists could now select either hotel or have a week at both.

As the post-war austerity conditions diminished the company commenced 'signing up' various other local hotels acting as booking agents on their behalf. Three hotels in Shetland joined the scheme in 1955 and were all serviced by the *St. Magnus* (III) with her considerable passenger capacity. One hotel was on the island of Unst and this required 'cruisers' to transfer to the *Earl of Zetland* (II) to reach their destination. In 1956 the *St. Clair* (III) was brought into the range of holidays offered and five hotels participated that year. In 1957 an additional hotel was offered and it remained at five or six until 1965, although there were seven in 1959. In addition the two principal North Company hotels at Hillswick and Stenness continued to be served by the *St. Ninian* (II). Apart from all these inclusive cruise/hotel holidays, it was always possible to undertake the round trip on some of the ships as a pure cruise. These were certainly available from 1902 on selected vessels and from 1950 were available on any of the passenger vessels and from 1955 included the cargo vessels (12 passengers) as well. One trip which was very popular was the mini-cruise though this descriptive title was not used until 1972. Their origin can be traced back as far as 1898, although at that time they could only be arranged on a stage by stage basis and involved a main line vessel to Lerwick before transferring to the *Earl of Zetland* and returning similarly. From 1946 the mini-cruise was offered as an all inclusive the *St. Clair/Earl of Zetland* package and the basic concept exists to this day, albeit without the North Isles extension, employing the ro-ro ferries.

The *St. Clair* (III) at Lerwick. The ship entered service in 1960 and was the last passenger-only ship on the Orkney and Shetland routes. *(Author's collection)*

The company had been considering a new ship for some time, one which can perhaps be considered an 'intermediate' vessel, as her design was for only 50 passengers and she was envisaged as the Caithness steamer with her other main role being to relieve the main line vessels when they were off on annual refit. Perhaps the additional trade anticipated during the construction of the various nuclear installations at Dounreay, only a few miles west of Scrabster, had influenced this decision. Whatever the reason, the design was significantly altered after the order was placed. What appeared in 1955 was a large cargo vessel with cabins for 12 passengers, eight of which were single-berth, an innovation in the fleet. This was the *St. Rognvald* (III) and she introduced a completely new profile to the fleet with all aft

47

superstructure. There was a large deckhouse amidships extending from side to side and this incorporated store-rooms, the cargo refrigerating machines and, most importantly, the access for the cattle ramp which linked the shelter deck with the 'tween deck. Unlike the *St. Clement* (II), this cattle ramp could be rigged at either side of the ship to suit loading requirements, though it was almost permanently rigged on the starboard side. Another innovatory feature was a heavy lift derrick for 15 tons, the other five derricks being for 3 or 5 tons.

Both holds were fitted for livestock carriage and there was a portable ramp installed to load livestock into Number 2 hold, something which previously had only been fitted to the *St. Ninian* (II). The *St. Rognvald* (III) largely took over the duties of the *St. Clement* (II) and normally spent September/October on livestock traffic which saw her visiting Baltasound and Fetlar occasionally, as well as the main ports. During the winter she operated what was effectively the secondary indirect service vessel, while the *St. Magnus* (III) was relieving on other routes. In the spring and summer she normally operated a freight service to Kirkwall, St. Margaret's Hope (fortnightly) and Stromness.

On the introduction of the *St. Rognvald* (III), the *Amelia* was withdrawn and scrapped and the *Rora Head* generally covered Cooper's freight service, sometimes loading in Leith at both Cooper's and the North Company berth. In 1956 the Caithness service was withdrawn due to high operating expenses and the *Rora Head* was sold to Lerwick owners. The *St. Clement* (II) had also taken over some of the Cooper's sailings and it was around this time that Cooper's shed and office at Leith was relinquished and all the traffic concentrated at the Victoria Dock complex. It was also around 1954 that the company started the practice of calling at non-standard Orkney ports during March/April. About 4/5

The St Clair (III) *dressed overall on her maiden voyage.* **(Author's collection)**

sailings would be made calling at Stronsay, Sanday and Westray, and occasionally Longhope, normally combined with Caithness or Stromness sailings. The *Amelia* was employed in 1954, the *Rora Head* 1956 and the *St. Clement* thereafter for about a decade. Cargoes were invariably manufactured manures and feeding stuffs for livestock. By 1956 with the introduction of the *St. Rognvald* (III), the sale of the 61-year-old *Amelia* and the 35-year-old *Rora Head*, the fleet was reduced to seven ships with the average was now 13 years. This included the elderly *St. Magnus* (III) which had

The *St. Magnus* (IV) arriving at Leith in March 1966. *(Author's collection)*

been built in 1924. However, when the *St. Rognvald* (III) joined the fleet, the opportunity was taken to modernise the *St. Magnus* (III) and she was withdrawn from service for three months (February-May 1956) and was converted to being an oil-burning vessel. The Second Class and crews' accommodation was remodelled from dormitory style to cabins. The First Class accommodation was less affected but the 18-berth ladies' cabin was converted to two 4-berth and one 6-berth cabins, and additional showers and toilet facilities were also installed. Like many of the earlier ships, some of the 'tween deck spaces were convertible, i.e. First Class cabins in summer, livestock accommodation in winter! On the *St. Magnus* (III) this latterly consisted of a block of twelve 2-berth cabins (converted from dormitory style earlier)

and these were altered to provide four 4-berth and eight 2-berth cabins. (These cabins were forever known to the crew as the 'cattle stalls' with the resultant entertainment of the occupants when they found out.) A further two 2-berth cabins were built on the shelter deck amidships. These alterations still provided berths for 224 First Class passengers, only ten less than originally built arrangement.

Another main line vessel joined the fleet in 1960 in the form of the *St. Clair* (III) and although significantly larger (3,302 tons) than the *St. Ninian* (II), perhaps surprisingly, was a reversion to single screw. She had a more 'built-up' profile than anything previously, and reverted to the two holds forward and one aft. The four deck infrastructure allowed cabins to be located higher with all First Class completely above the waterline. The dining saloon was located aft of the engine casing, reverting to the shelter deck, thus at the same level as her namesake. First Class cabins were distributed over four decks and consisted of four 4-berth and eighty-two 2-berth. As with the *St. Ninian* (II), the Second Class was located in the forward section of the

The *St. Magnus* (V) (ex *City of Dublin*) departing from Aberdeen for Leith on her maiden voyage for the company on 4th June 1967. *(A W McRobb)*

Before the ro-ro ferry; loading a coach on the *St. Rognvald* (III) at Stromness in 1966. (*Author's collection*)

The *St. Clement* (II) of 1946 at Scrabster. (*Author's collection*)

midships superstructure. Her namesake had been renamed the *St. Clair II* some time earlier and the introduction of the new *St. Clair* (III) resulted in the *St. Magnus* (III) being sold for scrap. The *St. Clair II* was then renamed *St. Magnus* (IV). The new *St. Clair* (III) took up the direct Aberdeen-Lerwick route, while the *St. Magnus* (IV) transferred to the secondary indirect route.

In 1961 the fortnightly call to St. Margaret's Hope had been reduced to a call every third week and 3rd May 1966 marked the withdrawal of calling there. The entire fleet was affected by the lengthy seamen's strike between mid-May and the beginning of July although the *St. Rognvald* (III) had been allowed to make a few trips with emergency supplies. The first ship to resume sailing was the *Earl of Zetland* (II)

(Lerwick-Kirkwall-Aberdeen), bringing down the 'North' company seafarers to crew the fleet which was laid up in Aberdeen and Leith.

Towards the end of 1966 it was announced that the *St. Magnus* (IV) was to be withdrawn and would be replaced by a cargo/livestock vessel. The *St. Magnus* (IV) was renamed the *St. Magnus II* in October and she is unusual in having operated under six different names under the one ownership: *St. Clair*, HMS *Baldur*, *St. Clair*, *St. Clair* II, *St. Magnus*, and *St. Magnus II*. Her replacement was the *City of Dublin* (Palgrave/Murphy) which was overhauled and converted for North Company service at Ardrossan over six months and entered service on 30th March 1967 from Leith on the secondary indirect service. She had been renamed the *St.*

Magnus (V) a fortnight earlier and at a distance was almost indistinguishable from the *St. Rognvald* (III). The main line fleet was now down to only two vessels. This also resulted in the contraction of the cruise/hotel programme, only three hotels being signed up for the 1967 and 1968 seasons, although the *St. Ninian* (II) continued additionally to serve Hillswick and Stenness.

An unusual situation occurred in February 1970 when the *St. Clair* (V) was chartered to relieve the Liverpool-Belfast service for about two weeks while the *Ulster Queen* and the *Ulster Prince* were on survey. This arrangement was repeated in 1971 but covered four weeks and was facilitated by the fact that both companies were part of the Coast Lines Group which had taken over the North Company in 1961.

Early in September 1970 the company had discussed their plans with the local island authorities for the restructuring of the fleet and services. This envisaged three ro-ro vessels, one each for the Pentland Firth, Lerwick and Kirkwall routes, the last one being a 12-passenger vessel, but none would be in service before 1975. In addition Leith would be closed down and the *St. Ninian* (II) would be withdrawn. Stromness (apart from the Pentland Firth sailings) would also fall victim, all of these changes targeted for early 1971.

The final scheduled Stromness call was made on 24th February 1971 by the *St. Clement* (II), but it was stated that calls would be made if inducements were favourable. It appears there were a few infrequent isolated calls . The *St. Magnus* (V) made the final sailing from Leith on 9th March 1971. The *St. Ninian* (II) which was relieving the *St. Clair* (V) made her last sailing when she arrived in Aberdeen on 28th February and was subsequently sold to Canadian interests, leaving Aberdeen on 26th April 1971 with basically a North Company crew for the delivery voyage. From this time the Lerwick service continued to operate from Matthew's Quay, but Orkney freight services were transferred to Jamieson's Quay which was the Coast Lines complex and the basic pattern became:

The *St. Rognvald* ex Aberdeen (Mondays), Kirkwall (Tuesdays), Lerwick (Wednesdays), for Aberdeen (arr Thursdays).

The *St. Clement* ex Aberdeen (Tuesdays), Kirkwall (Wednesdays/Thursdays), Aberdeen (arr Fridays)

The *St. Magnus* ex Aberdeen (Tuesdays), Kirkwall (weekend), Aberdeen (arr Tuesday).

While this appeared to be poor utilisation of vessels, it eliminated expensive weekend discharging of cargo and the three vessels were basically required in that the *St. Clement* (II) normally spent 10 weeks in the summer assisting with car traffic on the Pentland Firth and many additional sailings would be required during the autumn livestock season while allowances had to be made for the annual refits of all six vessels. During 1971 only the *St. Clair* (V) was advertised in the summer season brochure, but 1972 saw a reversion to the indirect service being promoted (either the *St. Rognvald* (III) or the *St. Clement* (II), depending on whether early or late summer) and from May 1972 this sailing included a Kirkwall call southbound, arriving Aberdeen on Friday. A further contraction was the sale of the St. Magnus Hotel, Hillswick around May 1972, the Stenness Hotel having been sold as far back as 1953 although still included in the holiday packages up to 1970.

In October 1972 home and overseas yards had been requested to tender for the proposed Aberdeen-Lerwick ro-ro ferry, while, finally, the Pentland Firth ro-ro ferry contract was announced on 12th December to be built by Hall Russell, Aberdeen and with delivery expected in spring 1974.

In perhaps the worst mishap since the war, the *St.*

The *St. Ola* (III) at Scrabster on 28th January 1975, her first call on a special proving voyage prior to entering commercial service. (*A W McRobb*)

Rognvald (III) ran aground on Thieves Holm (Kirkwall Bay) on 4th May 1973 and was refloated on the 18th. As the *St. Ola* (II) was off on refit at the time, the *Clarity* was chartered for about two weeks until her return. The *St. Rognvald* (III) returned to service on 25th June.

The Aberdeen-Lerwick ro-ro ferry was eventually ordered in July 1973 with delivery from Hall Russell's at Aberdeen in May 1975, but the shipyard subsequently withdrew from the

contract citing pressure of other work and it was back to square one. Coast Lines had been taken over by the P & O Group in February 1971 and with the greater flexibility that this allowed, a fresh look was taken on the requirements for the Lerwick ferry. Two vessels were considered in late 1974, the *Lion* (Burns & Laird) and the *Norwave* (North Sea Ferries).

The new Pentland Firth vessel, the first ro-ro ferry in the

fleet, the *St. Ola* (III) was launched at Aberdeen on 24th January 1974 with delivery programmed for mid-June. It emerged that the first choice of name had been the *St. Olaf*, perpetuating the name of the first North Company vessel to operate on the route, but that name was unavailable. In preparation for the arrival of the new ferry the existing vessel on the route had been renamed the *St. Ola II*. The new *St. Ola* visited the Firth of Forth in mid-September for drydocking and speed trials and carried out final trials in Aberdeen Bay on 29th October 1974, later sailing overnight to Stromness. By arrangement she met up with the *St. Ola II* off Houton (near Stromness) at 09.00 the next morning subsequently berthing at the linkspan. An official reception was held on board for local dignatories on the arrival day and the *St. Ola* (III) was open to the public on 31st October. On 1st November local schoolchildren were granted a special holiday and 420 visited the new ship. However, the delays at the shipyard paled into insignificance compared with the delays at Scrabster where the terminal was nowhere near ready. The *St. Ola* (III) lay unused for three months at Stromness before entering service.

Another part of the operations which had been seeing significant changes was on the North Isles of Shetland. In the summer of 1970 Zetland County Council received approval for their inter-island car ferry service which would attract a 75% Government Grant. At that stage this required four vessels and ten purpose built terminals, although a fifth vessel (spare) was later added to the initial concept. The *Earl of Zetland* (II) was 31 years old and replacement by another conventional vessel was not a realistic option. The first of Zetland County Council's ferries, the *Fivla*, entered service on 21st May 1973 between Toft (mainland) and Ulsta (Yell), and after a transitional period, the *Earl of Zetland* (II) progressively dropped her various calling ports in the North

The St. Ola (III) was the first roll on-roll off ferry for the Pentland Firth crossing. (*Author's collection*)

Isles as each new ferry was introduced. Calls at Mid Yell (normally Thursdays) and Cullivoe, Yell (Fridays only) were discontinued after 1st August 1973, while final calls at Uyeasound, Unst (Mondays/Tuesdays overnight and Wednesdays, Fridays/Saturdays) and Baltasound, Unst (Fridays/Saturdays overnight) were made on 14th and 15th December respectively. The latter two ports were actually 'closed' by the *St. Ola II* which was on relief duties at the time. The overnight stopovers which had been part of the North Isles history since 1877, terminated after 97 years, not quite making their century. From 17th December 1973, a new pattern of services commenced:

Mondays only Lerwick 0800 - Whalsay, Skerries, Fetlar, Whalsay, Lerwick (arr c. 17.00).

Wednesdays only Lerwick 0900 - Whalsay - Lerwick (arr c.12.00)

Fridays only Lerwick 10.00 - Whalsay, Fetlar, Whalsay, Lerwick (arr. c.17.00)

On 22nd November the final Fetlar call was made.

In June 1974 the *Ortolan* (G & M division of P & O) appeared on an inter-group charter and assisted the *St. Clair* (V) with freight trips. However, the first practical signs of the North Company's involvement with North Sea oil, was imminent when she made a number of trips to Flotta (which eventually became the ELF oil terminal) and also called at Lyness. The *Ortolan* appears to have been employed intermittantly until mid-December.

Roll On - Roll Off : The First Generation

On 26th January 1975 the new *St. Ola* (III) made a circumnavigation of Hoy for crew familiarisation purposes to test all machinery systems. On 28th she made a VIP's crossing to Scrabster and on the following day she made her maiden voyage from Stromness to Scrabster. At long last ro-ro had come to fruition, some eleven years after its introduction in MacBrayne territory in the Western Isles. With her better speed, some schedule adjustments were made and were ex Stromness 08.45, ex Scrabster 12.00 (formerly 08.30/13.00). Internally the passenger accommodation was confined to the shelter (or upper deck) with a large observation saloon at the fore and a cafeteria/bar at the after end which was divided down the centre line on an open-plan layout. An entrance foyer and purser's office was amidships. Vehicles had the use of th entire main deck with two wing decks above accessed by lifts and frequently used for livestock.

The *St. Ola II* departed for Aberdeen on 29th January

1975 and after a few days was sold for use as a seismic survey vessel. Less than a month later the *Earl of Zetland* made her final voyage on 21st February. As a mark of the close relationship between the ship and the community, the crew on the *Earl of Zetland* held a private dinner party on board that evening and a few days later were the guests of the Provost at a recption in Lerwick Town Hall. A week later she left Lerwick for Aberdeen, played out by the town band, and was sold for further work as a seismic research vessel. Latterly she had been serving Whalsay and Skerries only and Zetland County Council took over the Skerries route from the end of February 1975. While all five of the Zetland County Council ferries had now been delivered, there were no terminals ready at Symbister (Whalsay) or Laxo (mainland) to allow the Whalsay service to operate. Instead the *Grima* from the quintet was chartered by the North Company and provided a Symbister-Lerwick service until January 1976 when the Zetland County Council ferry service commenced. She was island based and the schedule was ex Symbister 09.00 Tuesdays only and 07.30/13.00 Fridays only and ex Lerwick 14.00 Tuesdays only and 10.00/16.30 Fridays only.

In March 1975, the *Lion* was put out to tender for conversion to become the Lerwick ferry, but mounting losses on P&O's long routes (Lisbon, Tangier and San Sebastian) forced a rethink and in October it was announced that the *SF Panther* (Southern Ferries of the P&O Group) would be employed instead! With what was effectively a five ship fleet which only included one ro-ro vessel, a relief vessel had to be chartered from outside. The *Clansman* (Caledonian MacBrayne) relieved the *St. Ola* during the first half of November that year and in fact fulfilled this role every year until 1982/3.

While the *St. Clair* and the three cargo ships continued

The *St Ola* (III) with the Old Man of Hoy and Pentland Firth beyond. *(P&O)*

The *St. Clair* (IV) leaving Aberdeen on 12th April 1982 with the P&O flag on her funnel. (*Author's collection*)

as before, the most significant change during that first year of ro-ro was that the Pentland Firth sailings were increased during the summer. The old *St. Ola* had operated extra summer crossings for many years, but these were invariably only as required and traffic patterns generally confined these to the Friday to Monday period while Sunday sailings had become part of the advertised schedule from 1959 (July/August only) onwards. From the beginning of June the

St. Ola (III) made an extra 15.00 Wednesdays only crossing from Stromness while on Thursdays five single crossings, commencing at 08.45 from Scrabster were provided until the end of August. This was mainly to provide a day excursion on Thursdays from the Caithness side but on a number of occasions the Wednesday evening service was employed for charter cruises along the coast or through Scapa Flow and this arrangement continued for a number of years.

At the beginning of October 1975 the North Company title disappeared, the company initially trading as P&O Ferries (Orkney & Shetland Services) and the *St. Ola* reappeared from refit in November with P&O pale blue funnels, the first of the visual alterations.

During 1974 preliminary site work at Lerwick had commenced for the Aberdeen and Lerwick ro-ro terminals though the construction phase did not commence until 1976 at Aberdeen and effectively became an extension of the then current Kirkwall freight berths. In the same month all vessels commenced using the new Lerwick facilities at Holmsgarth except for the *St. Clair* (III) which continued to use the 'mail' berth at Victoria Pier. The Matthews Quay complex at Aberdeen was finally vacated at the end of October with the *St. Clair* transferring to a temporary berth at Regent's Quay.

In 1975 indications that North Sea oil was to be a major force, particularly in the northern North Sea, resulted in the freight only ro-ro vessel, the *Helga*, being purchased by P&O for management by the North Company. She was renamed the *Rof Beaver* (Rof signifying 'roll-on freighter'), the 'Beaver' being in accord with P&O's then stated policy of using the Burns' fleets animal names for all their ferries. She was Leith based and with no North Company presence there by then, agents were appointed to look after her. She carried no

The *Rof Beaver* leaving Leith in August 1975. (*Author's collection*)

passengers and the accommodation block was sited right aft. Loading was via the stern ramp and there was a large hold beneath the vehicle deck which could be conventionally crane loaded. She was overhauled in Marseilles and made her delivery voyage to Immingham in May, loading for Sullom Voe. During that first year she visited Peterhead, Belfast, Stromness, Sandwick (Shetland) and Lerwick, as well as her more frequent visits to Flotta and Sullom Voe. She even got as far as Rotterdam on one occasion!

The *Ortolan* was again also frequently employed on charter, obviously on oil-related work and she visited Leith, Inverkeithing, Dundee, Peterhead, Flotta, Kirkwall, Sandwick and Sullom Voe. Sister vessel the *Oriole* also made a few appearances apparently on traditional North Company

The *St. Magnus* (VI) with a black hull and pale blue funnels. The roll on - roll off freight vessel took up service in 1978 after previously having been chartered as the *Dorset*. *(Author's collection)*

routes from Aberdeen to Kirkwall and Lerwick.

In the Islands there was continuous criticism of the 'blue' funnels which became more vociferous at the thought that their cherished 'Saint' names could disappear to be replaced with 'animal' names, but this criticism was allayed when an announcement was made that the *SF Panther* would be renamed the *St. Clair* (IV). The blue funnels remained but the 'Beaver' was to be the only 'animal' to enter the fleet list.

The *Rof Beaver's* stern ramp allowed her to discharge on to a quayside which she invariably did at Leith and she was the first vessel to use the Lerwick linkspan in June 1976. She largely confined herself to Lerwick and Sullom Voe sailings, but did make single calls at Lyness and Middlesborough. There were many more inter-group charters that year, principally the *Ortolan*, visiting London on one occasion with the *Petrel* and the *Dorset Coast* also making appearances. One non-P&O vessel to be chartered was the *Rosemarkie* which briefly appeared, apparently on traditional freight work. At the beginning of December 1976, the *St Clement*, the smallest of the frieght ships, was sold to the Greeks.

With the entry into service of *St.Clair* (IV) on the 4th April 1977, Shetland now had full ro-ro services to the outside world. A new lower fares structure from the islands, (southbound), was introduced at this time. The *St. Clair II* (III) continued to make some freight sailings including two Indirect route sailings, relieving the *St. Rognvald* (III) and making rare calls at Kirkwall. She finished early in June, being sold on as the *Al Khairat* to the Meat Foodstuff Company of Kuwait.

The *St. Ola* (III) had a breakdown at the start of 1977, running on reduced power at first, and missing some sailings if the weather was poor. The *St.Magnus* (V) was called in to take some cars south from Kirkwall to Aberdeen, (New Year holiday traffic) while the *St. Rognvald* (III) helped out with an extra crossing of the Pentland Firth. In May 1977 the *St. Magnus* (V) was sold on to Sun Star Lines of Limassol Cyprus.as the *Mitera Eirina*. The *Ortolan* and the *Petrel* had again helped out on the freight side in September 1976, with the *Petrel* again in June 1977. The *Lairdsfox*, and the *Dorset Coast* also appeared in June 1977, and from July to September 1978. In September 1977 the *Ortolan* finished with the P&O. Group.

Livestock sailings by chartered tonnage on an annual seasonal basis commenced with the *Angus Express* on 17th September 1977. This situation was as a result of the

The *St. Ola* (IV) at Scrabster with the cliffs of Caithness behind. (*Ian Somerville*)

introduction of ro-ro operations and the demise of the *St. Magnus* (V) and the *St. Clement* (II). This arrangement continues to the present day, for periods of one to three months annually. These livestock sailings have gradually ceased making local calls within both island groups, concentrating on Lerwick (Shetland) and Kirkwall (Orkney). Aberdeen is the principal mainland port, but Invergordon and Peterhead have been used occasionally.

The *Bussard*, a Danish ship, was chartered for 3-4 weeks for sevices from Aberdeen to Kirkwall, sometimes extending the service to Lerwick. The ro ro freighter *Dorset* appeared on charter in February 1978 to relieve on the freight side on the Pentland Firth after which P&O (Orkney and Shetland Services) decided to purchase her and to send her to Belfast for refit. She took up services in the North with the name the *St. Magnus* (VI) on the Indirect service, substituting Stromness for Kirkwall, immediately causing consternation with the authorities in Kirkwall who saw a need for a linkspan to retain links with Aberdeen and the south! The *Dorset* was built as the *Donautal* in 1970.

The *St. Magnus* started a Scandinavian service to Hanstholm in Denmark, and Kristiansand in Norway. A regular pattern emerged which fitted in with her other duties while the *St. Rognvald* (III) was sold to Naviera Winton S/A Panama as the *Winston*.

A chartered Norwegian vessel the *Nornan Fjord*, brought in animal feedstuffs to the islands over a ten day period while the following year she reappeared as the *Sea Fisher*, (Fishers of Barrow), to relieve the *St. Magnus*. The *Condor* also appeared for a month to help out.

Fares were increased in March 1980 and brought a change to the rebate system, an increase on the passage subsidy and also a subsidy for accompanied cars from the islands.

A second linkspan, the Eurolink, in Aberdeen Harbour was used by one of the charter ships and was to be used by company ships on occasions over the years.

The Highlands and Islands Development Board (HIDB) was set up to promote development in the Highland area and produced a report suggesting that Scrabster should be the port for Shetland. However this was not acceptable to the Shetlanders who campaigned to keep the Aberdeen connection.

When the *St. Magnus* was overhauled in 1982 some Orkney bound freight was sent by road to Scrabster from Aberdeen. This set a trend for the future and road improvements north of Inverness reduced the overall journey times to the Caithness port.

The *Smyril,* a car and passenger ro-ro ferry of Strandfaraskip Landsin (Faroese Government Shipping Department), was used to relieve the *St. Magnus* which in turn relieved the *St. Clair*. The *St. Magnus* made a trip for the *Rof Beaver* on 1st March 1982 incorporating a return visit to Leith.

In May 1982 the *St. Clair* was used for a fund-raising event for the Lerwick Lifeboat and this became an annual event, as did the cruise around Bressay and the bird sanctuary at Noss. The *Earl of Zetland* had previously made this cruise on similar charters during the fifties!

In autumn 1982 the *Smyril* relieved the *St. Clair*, followed by the *St. Ola*. The *Smyril* had to return to the Faroes before the *St. Ola*'s refit was complete and the *St. Magnus* took over for the short time until the *St. Ola* was able to return to her route. A fire aboard the *St. Ola* delayed her return and the *St. Magnus* was then assisted by the *Rof Beaver* and the *Orcadia* when she was available. In late November the *Clansman* of Caledonian MacBrayne was called in to cover the route. In January the *Clansman* had to return to service on the West Coast and the interim arrangements were resumed i.e. the *St. Magnus*, the *Rof Beaver* and the *Orcadia* working the route between them until the *St. Ola* resumed service on 7th February 1983. During this time when the *Orcadia* was on the Pentland Firth she sailed from Kirkwall to Scrabster but on at least two occasions she called at Wick.

The *Penn Ar Bed* (Brittany Ferries) relieved the *St. Clair* for two weeks in February 1983.

On 9th May there was an unusual sailing. to Gothenburg by the *St. Clair* for the final of the European Cup Winners Football Cup (Aberdeen versus Real Madrid) which Aberdeen won. A mini-cruise to Bergen took place in September 1983.

The St. Ola's next relief was carried out in 1984, as because of her fire the previous certificate had been issued in the spring of 1983, and from then on her overhaul was in the January- February period. (British passenger ships require to be given an annual survey and certification). The St. Magnus was given a passenger certificate for 50 passengers on the Pentland Firth crossing so she was used now regularly to relieve the St. Ola.

The Smyril was again used for relief duties in 1984 for two weeks at which time the St. Clair was refitted with extra cabins. During May the ship offered a mini-cruise to Harlingen in Holland.

The Norrona owned by Smyril Lines (a Faroese privatised company), had replaced the Smyril on the link between Faroe, Shetland and Norway in June 1983 and in 1985 they advertised through links to Britain using P&O (Orkney and Shetland Services) as their UK agents.

The Highlands and Islands Development Board and Orkney Council assisted some local shareholders to set up a new company, Viking Island Ferries, to operate a service linking Orkney with Shetland. They chose Kirkwall, Westray and Scalloway as their ports. The Devoniun ex Scillonian II was the ship chosen. She arrived at Westray from Torquay on 17th November 1985 and visited Kirkwall the following day and was renamed the Syllingar. The ship made her maiden voyage on 15th December but the service suffered from breakdowns and weather problems and by May 1986 the company was in receivership.

Ro-Ro : Daily sailings to Shetland!

P&O announced at this time, that they would acquire a second passenger ship/ferry to operate the Aberdeen, Stromness, Lerwick route and additional direct sailings between Aberdeen and Lerwick.

The nf Panther, formerly of P&O Normandy Ferries' Dover - Boulogne route, was purchased by the company. Built as the Djursland for Jydsk Faergesfart of Denmark in 1971, the contract to refit her was awarded to Hall Russell's Aberdeen shipyard. The ship was refitted as an overnight ferry with cabins forward on main and upper decks.with restaurant, shop, TV room and bar from aft of mid ships.on the main deck. A self service restaurant-cum cinema aft doubles up with reclining seats as the overnight lounge on the upper deck, with more cabins on the port side aft.

The proposed pattern of services was: Mondays to Friday evenings departures northbound and southbound on Sundays to Thursdays with an additional Saturday midday sailing northbound via Orkney. The Friday sailing southbound was to leave Lerwick at midday via Orkney. The St. Clair would take the Monday, Wednesday and Friday northbound sailings while the second ship would take the Tuesday, Thursday and Saturday northbound sailings. Sailings on a daily basis to Shetland for passengers had returned.

In 1986 the Orcadia was chartered to P&O to operate a weekly inter-island service from Kirkwall to Scalloway and on occasion diverted to Lerwick.

The St. Magnus continued on the Rof Beaver's roster until the nf Panther was ready for service. Plans were made to have more mini-cruises for the spring and autumn when the new ship took up the routes but the St. Clair eventually undertook most of them. Mrs Olivia Ford renamed the nf Panther, the St. Sunniva on 27th March 1987. The bridge wings were damaged on the maiden voyage and electrical problems resulted in the ship having to return to Aberdeen but the special party of invited guests were given a later opportunity to sail on the St. Sunniva. A decision to use

The *St Clair* (V) leaves Aberdeen in May 1998. The vessel was built in Germany in 1971 and was formerly the *Travemunde*, *Njegos* and *Tregastel*. Following purchase and a major refit in 1992, she was switched to the P&O Scottish Ferries' Shetland link. *(Miles Cowsill)* stronger glass in all forward windows was made after this voyage!

In 1987 the brochure had a 2-page feature on the 150th Anniversary of P&O with various events taking place e.g.opening of the Bod of Gremista (birthplace of Arthur Anderson, founder of P&O Company), two visits to Leith on consecutive weekends, and an Orkney week promotion was held in Aberdeen.

The *St. Magnus* now regularly used the EuroLink. She was chartered to the Ministry of Defence in November 1987 when she sailed toto Loch Ryan in south west Scotland. The *St. Sunniva* became the relief vessel for the fleet from 1988 onwards.

Plans to visit the Glasgow Garden Festival in summer 1988 were announced in the autumn of 1987. The *St.Sunniva's* Glasgow visit was incorporated with a northbound sailing (direct) to Lerwick, returning to Stromness, before cruising through the Western Isles to Glasgow. Due to industrial action the passengers had to be flown north after an extended visit to the Garden Festival, where the ship was at an on quay site.

In January 1989 the Company changed the title of their North services once again when P&O Scottish Ferries was adopted. P&O took over their own dock labour staff on the demise of the National Dock Labour Scheme.

In 1989 the *St. Magnus's* freight sailings to and from Leith were altered to Grangemouth for 6/8 weeks while the dock gates in Leith were being repaired.

The *St. Clair* made a mini cruise to Maloy in Norway in spring 1989. At this time she was involved with further safety excercises involving Lifeboat, Coastguard, Military personnel as guinea pigs, to test evacuation procedures. The *St. Clair* and later the *St. Ola* came under close scrutiny as the costs of new safety measures, said to be in the order of £335,000

for the passenger fleet, were implemented following the *Herald Of Free Enterprise* ferry disaster. It was suggested by company officials that the *Norrona* should be bought to replace the *St. Clair*.

The *St.Sunniva* added mid week northbound calls each Tuesday at Stromness during the peak season leaving Aberdeen at midday and Lerwick at midday on Wednesdays. This was linked with a call of about an hour and a half in each direction at Stromness, from 1989.

A freight service to Hanstholm (Denmark), was again suggested in 1988.and an additonal freight ship was required for this service, so a charter of the *Marino Torre* from Italian owners took place in 1989. She had fifty per cent more freight capacity than *St. Magnus* so she was eventually bought in as her successor on the Indirect service. She was renamed the *St. Rognvald* (IV) which had been built as the *Rhonetal* in 1970 at Lubeck, Germany

The *St. Magnus* (VI) was relieved by the *Juniper* of Limassol in July 1989 before leaving for a charter on the Southampton to Cherbourg service and being offered for sale. The *Smyril* was chartered briefly to operate the new Scandinavian link and also operated on the Stromness to Lerwick service while the *St. Magnus* was away. A second hand replacement for the *St. Clair* was now planned and £15 million set aside for this purpose.

The *St. Clair* took part in the Forth Bridge Centenary celebrations opened officially by HRH Prince Edward who switched on the floodlighting.

Mr. Graeme Dunlop was brought into manage this northern outpost for one year while Eric Turner became Chairman of Lloyd's Register of Shipping (Scotland).

During the overhaul period in 1992 the *St. Rognvald* was damaged in heavy weather requiring to be towed to Aberdeen when the *Smyril* was chartered for a week to cover. During this

The *St.Sunniva* (III) seen in the evening light with Mousa broch in the background. *(Charles Tait)*

The *St. Rognvald* (IV) at Lerwick during her weekend lay-over at the port in May 1998. (*Miles Cowsill*)

time she combined the rosters of both the *St. Sunniva* and the *St. Rognvald* At this time it was announced that the *Smyril* would operate to Aberdeen on its Faroese service in lieu of Scrabster.

In 1991 the link had been maintained by the *Teistin*, another Faroese Government ship.

Ro-Ro: The Second Generation

The *Tregastel* of Brittany Ferries was bought in 1991 to commence service in 1992. She was sent to the Lloyd Werft yard at Bremerhaven for conversion work to be done. The *St. Ola* (III) was to be replaced by the *Eckero* ex *Svea Scarlett*, of Eckero Lines of Finland.

The Stromness berth was proving too short for both the *St. Sunniva* and the *St. Rognvald* and so work was put in hand to extend it. While this was being done the *St Sunniva* served Kirkwall in lieu of Stromness on some sailings and the *St. Rognvald* made additional calls there-in addition to her Monday calls. The *St Ola* spent more time at Scrabster, sometimes on 'light' sailings as well as others already timetabled.

In the summer of 1991 the Tall Ships' Race was staged at Aberdeen and the.*St. Sunniva* was used by V.I.P's reviewing the fleet cruise.

In 1992 the *Tregastel* joined the fleet as *St. Clair* (V) Built as the *Travemunde* in 1971 for Moltzau Line (predecessors of Gedser - Travemunde Ruten), with a gross tonnage of 4,231, she has four passenger decks , and two car/vehicle decks and was the largest ship in the fleet. The passenger cabins were mainly on C and D decks, the bar, lounges, restaurant, childrens' play area, ships office on B deck, and the reclining seat lounge on A deck.

In preparation her her own replacement on the Pentland Firth service, the *St. Ola* was given the suffix 'II' before

retiring to Leith on the sale list. The *St. Clair* (IV) was also given the prefix 'II' but on 26th February 1992 was sold to Malaysian interests. Before entering service the *St. Ola* (IV) visited Kirkwall on a 'show the flag' cruise. As visits had been made to Scapa Pier by previous incumbents of the name, this was an unusual occurrence. Stromness and Scrabster visits and berthing trials then followed and the *St. Ola* (IV) entered service on Wednesday 25th March 1992 The main deck has a television lounge forward, ship's office in the foyer, restaurant and shop while the bar is on the upper deck. She was built by Jos L. Meyer at Papenburg in 1971 as the *Svea Scarlett*. Of 2,967 gross tons, the ship is is 86.3 metres (283ft.) long, has a service speed of 17 knots and carries 500 passengers and up to 180 cars and or 20 commercial vehicles. As the *Cecilia*, the old *St. Ola* (III) was chartered to Svenska Rederi A.B., for a Denmark to Sweden crossing but was eventually sold to Greek owners.

The *St. Ola* (IV) made her first visit to Lerwick after the *St. Sunniva* had an engine failure and was grounded at Stromness. She made her crossing on Saturday evening arriving on Sunday morning and leaving an hour or so later, reaching Stromness in the late afternoon and taking up her Scrabster sailings in the evening. Her return sailing was cancelled on the occasions this happened.

When it was announced that the *Norrona's* calls at Lerwick were to cease at the end of August 1992, pressure from the Local Authority, Tourist Board and others which led to a decision to send the *St. Clair* to Bergen in the high season of

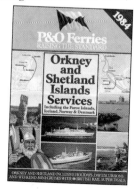

The *St. Ola* (IV) leaves Stromness to allow the *St. Sunniva* (III) to use the berth in June 1999. (*John May*)

1993. This used the Friday departure from Aberdeen at 18.00 to Lerwick, departing from Lerwick during late Saturday mornings for Bergen arriving at 22.00 local time with the return sailing to Lerwick and Aberdeen two hours later. This renewed a link with the past when the North Company had offered Norwegian sailings for twenty three years until 1908. This sevice continued in June, July and August for the next three years with slight timetable adjustments.

The *St Rognvald* (IV) was the relief vessel in most winters, releasing the *St. Sunniva* in the January to March period, to relieve the *St. Ola* (IV) and, the *St. Clair* (V) to have their own overhauls. The St. Rognvald was usually overhauled first for a week or so, and the *St. Sunniva* made her own regular sailings to clear backlogs in traffic which occur each year.

The *St. Rognvald* was chartered to Ferrymasters for their Middlesborough to Gothenburg service in 1993 and in 1994 she was chartered to Color Line for their Tyne to Bergen route. She continued with her own single weekly round trip to the Northern Isles during these years.

A report at this time suggested that a complete fleet replacement would cost around £100 million. Napier University suggested that using aluminium constructed catamarans, each costing £40 million, up to 800 passengers and 100 cars could be carried thereby saving up to two thirds of the journey time to Shetland.

In 1993 investigative reports for H.I.E. and Shetland Islands Council into more economic ways of providing ferry services to and from Aberdeen suggested that the Government provided and owned the ships, with P&O Scottish Ferries or others managing them.

MDS Transmodal produced a report for Orkney Islands Council into external ferry services to and from Orkney.

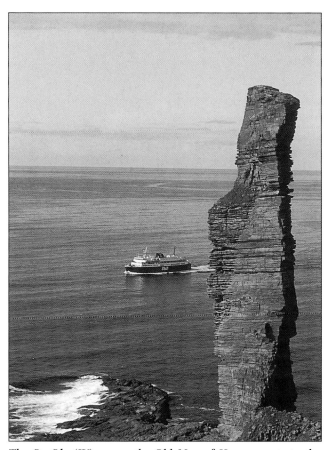

The *St. Ola* (IV) passes the Old Man of Hoy en-route to the mainland. (*Charles Tait*)

New terminal buildings for Stromness were planned in 1995, but were delayed and were to be built by the turn of the century. The Kirkwall office was moved into the pier buildings after they were renovated. New Safety Of Life At Sea regulations (SOLAS 90) implied that the *St. Ola* would require to be replaced by 2004 although initially the Company plans were to replace her in 2007.

Lifeline Tenders

A government proposal to put the services out to tender, came out in a report in 1995. Nineteen firms expressed an interest in tendering and eleven completed the tender documents although only five: Streamline Shipping, P&O Scottish Ferries, Orcargo and Stena maintained their interest. Orkney Ferries (Orkney Council through Orkney Islands Shipping Co. Ltd) were only interested in the Orkney service. Caledonian MacBrayne, the West Coast operators, were disallowed from applying to tender as they were considered to be an in house company, and the cost of any new ships would have to come from the public purse. P&O Scottish Ferries were awarded the contract for the "Lifeline services" from autumn 1997. The Tender documents giving the specification were published showing that livestock carrier arrangements were to continue, the June to August Pentland Firth service would operate thrice daily and twice daily for the other nine months, the June to August Aberdeen-Lerwick service would operate six times weekly and five times weekly in the other nine months, and an Orkney to Shetland weekly service would continue. The specification included a 95% target performance to be met.

The National Audit Office were poised to investigate the £11 million subsidy to P&O Scottish Ferries but a Scottish Office investigation into ferry pricing in Scotland took precedence. With a change of Government in 1997, a new tendering process was to be undertaken within the year to replace the current five year contract. Caledonian MacBrayne are asked to show whether they could enter this process "consistent with a suitable level of public subsidy." The Government set aside £50 million to fund the subsidy to P&O Scottish Ferries until the year 2002. Expression of interest in the tender process for the second contract was to be given by autumn 1998 and the successful tenderer was to be announced in spring 1999. To date no decision has been announced.

The *St. Sunniva* was used for the Annual.Coffee morning in 1995 as the *St. Clair* was having stability sponsons fitted during her annual refit. The *St. Rognvald* was used on the Pentland crossing on Sunday 30th June 1995 to take the cars and commercial vehicles as the *St. Ola* was off for urgent repairs. Passengers were bussed to John o Groats to make their crossing on the *Pentland Venture* (a passenger-only ferry) to Burwick, South Ronaldsay.

The Smyril Line announced that the *Norrona* would call at Lerwick again from 1998. P&O announced that they would withdraw from the Norwegian sailings. The *St. Clair*'s final Bergen sailing took place on 24th August 1997 and the seasonal service with the *Norrona* calling at Lerwick between the Faroes and Norway/Denmark resumed in 1998.

Diversions to Invergordon on at least two occasions in 1997 occurred when Aberdeen Harbour was closed . Four days of sailings were lost as both the *St. Clair* and the *St. Sunniva* who were involved on at least two occasions.

Local Artists had their work displayed on board the *St. Ola* in 1996 and 1997, and a function for the local Royal National Mission for Deep Sea Fishermen was held aboard at Scrabster.

A proposal to build three new ships was made by P&O Scottish Ferries depending on their successful gaining of the tender process. The ships would be built at the rate of one a year from 2000.

The *St. Clair* had problems with her variable pitch propellers during 1998. At first she took an additional four hours on the crossings and eventually had to go dry dock in Middlesborough for repairs. This meant that passengers had either to fly or wait a day to sail on the *St. Sunniva*. The additional hazard of fog meant some interesting journeys such as flying to Aberdeen then sailing on the *St. Sunniva* to travel from Orkney to Shetland. Some car traffic was carried on the *St. Rognvald* with passengers flying to or from Shetland.

A replacement floating dock was planned, to replace the existing dock on the north side of Holmsgarth terminal at Lerwick. The new dock was longer and so a contract was placed to extend the berth to aid berthing the ships in windy conditions. This dock will be able to accommodate any of the current fleet of P&O ships. Holmsgarth terminal was refurbished in 1998.

Short Sea Routes and other Contenders!

Short crossings of the Pentland Firth have looked attractive to many Orcadians, especially after the.Churchill Barriers were built. Passenger launches operating seasonal services between John O 'Groats and Burwick have built up a

The *St. Clair* outward bound from Lerwick to Aberdeen in May 1998. (*Miles Cowsill*)

steady business but are susceptible to poor weather. Day trips by coach and ferry to or from Inverness to mainland Orkney are a feature of this operation. Car ferry proposals on this short sea crossing over the years have given mild cause for concern to P&O Scottish Ferries. Orkney Island Council have shown interest at times and have been involved in reports and consultations on the subject.

Orkney Ferries plc. launched their ferry *Varagen* at Cochrane's of Selby. on 31st March 1989. The vessel made some test sailings but there were problems with the approach channels at both terminals and weight restrictions on the Orkney roads and so Orkney Island Shipping Company's ro-

ro facilities at Houton were tried after which the *Varagen* and the terminals were taken over by Orkney Island Council (OIC) under the auspices of Orkney Isles Shipping Company. An interim timetable was introduced from Mid August from Gills Bay to Houton. The Orkney Ferries' vessel *Varagen* had more problems with Gills Bay and a decision to lay her up was made. The linkspan was damaged and separated from its anchorages during storms in August 1989.

In 1990 Orcargo was formed to operate a mainly freight service between Invergordon and Kirkwall between five and six times a week. The advantage was to commercial traffic avoiding the Caithness roads at Berriedale and other notorious trouble spots. Additionally, restrictions on drivers' hours allowed journeys to the central belt of Scotland and back in one day. The Company provided the 40 metre long ro-ro vessel *Contender* (292 gross tons) with a certificate for twelve passengers and capable of carrying 12 artics or 130 cattle or 500 sheep. Orkney Island Council and Cromarty Ports Authority provided assistance to get this service up and running. Mounting losses during 1999 saw this service in the hands of the receiver.

Pentland Ferries, who had bought the *Iona* from Caledonian MacBrayne, were turned down by OIC for a loan of £300,000. They had hoped to start their service in July 1998 from Gills Bay to Burwick or St.Margaret's Hope, though an initial service using Scrabster was considered.

Acknowledgements

'Ferry Publications' express their very grateful thanks to Ian Somerville who has kindly given so much of his time adding material from Alastair McRobb's notes to finish the story of the company from 1974 onwards. His willingness to supply the missing chapters and his enthusiasm to see the book in print speak volumes for his respect and friendship for Alastair who was widely recognised as *the* authority on the 'North Boats.'

Coupled with Ian's work has been the invaluable assistance of both Alistair Deayton and Iain Quinn who are warmly thanked for the painstaking hours they spent sifting through Alastair's huge collection of slides, photographs and other memorabilia to produce suitable illustrations and captions for this publication.

Finally a debt of gratitude is due to Maureen McRobb for her enthusiastic support of this project, which included typing the complete manuscript from her husband's notes, and above all for her wish to see his lifelong passion in the 'North Boats' recorded in this permanent way.

Not only will this publication be eagerly awaited by the enthusiast fraternity (to which Alastair always provided such a thoroughly thoughtful and professional input and of which he was so much a part for so many years) but also to members of his family. Hopefully it will serve as a reminder of a special person and of his great love for the ships and the sea passages to the Northern Isles of Scotland.